Success in GCSE
Drama

Phil Parker and Craig Boardman

Folens

Dedications

To my family – for all their support and encouragement.
Phil

To Ruth – for showing me, when I was convinced otherwise, that stories can
have happy endings. Come what may…
Craig

United Kingdom: Folens Publishers, Apex Business Centre, Boscombe Road, Dunstable, LU5 4RL.
Email: folens@folens.com

Ireland: Folens Publishers, Greenhills Road, Tallaght, Dublin 24.
Email: info@folens.ie

Poland: JUKA, ul. Renesansowa 38, Warsaw 01-905

Editor: Geoff Tuttle

Layout artist: Jason Billin

Illustrations by Nomad Photography/Charlotte Bromley-Davenport.

Cover design: 2iDesign

First published 2005 by Folens Limited.

British Library Cataloguing in Publication Data. A catalogue record for this publication is available
from the British Library.

ISBN 1 84303 788 2

Contents

Acknowledgements

No work of this complexity is ever achieved in isolation. Both of us are indebted to the following people for help, advice and encouragement:

Mr Gardner, Head teacher of Colmers School and Sports College, for belief in us both and the practical support which came with that belief. Happy retirement Mike.

All the staff of Colmers School and Sports College for words of encouragement every time we kept dropping the 'book' into the conversation!

Jonothan Neelands, University of Warwick, for an afternoon of thoughts, challenges and insight which helped us make the last links in our planning.

Ruth Stockburn, from our Drama Department, for constant support, challenge and patience. Ruth encouraged us both from an early stage and readily gave her thoughts at each stage of the planning process.

Ellie Bunn, also from our Drama Department, for supporting us even when the deadlines came rushing upon us with the speed of a freight train.

We're lucky to have such a talented and diverse department and this book is a reflection of all of us who have worked at Colmers.

All of the drama teachers we have spoken to, casually or formally, who have given of their time and readily supplied their opinions on different aspects of this book. We have been amazed by the number of teachers in our area and beyond who have been so generous with their feedback. Thanks to all of them.

Peter Burton, our publisher, who heard the idea and went with it, giving us 'newbies' a lot of trust.

To Jason Billin for the amazing design work on this book. Our writing was just a collection of words but, with his work, he has made them speak volumes. Thank you.

To Geoff Tuttle, our unsung editor, who has put in more hours on this book than anyone would ever believe. His guidance, patience and outright professionalism has taken our rough stone and polished it into understanding. Many, many thanks.

Ian Wilson, our DVD designer, who has worked tirelessly to produce the outstanding disc accompanying this book.

To all our students, past and present, who constantly give us their ideas and thoughts on all the attempts we make to engage them in the learning of the subject that we believe in.

Finally, but not at all least, to Alice, Carly, Daniel, Keisha, Kerrie, Laura, Lianne, Matthew, Mickel, Rachael, Richard, Richard and Vicky. These thirteen students have helped to bring our ideas to life in the photographs and DVD for this book. They have been creative and generous in all they have done and have made this a better book by far.

For everyone involved in this book – we both hope you like the finished product and are proud of your involvement.

Any errors or omissions are entirely our own. (And were probably intended.)

Phil and Craig 2004

Introduction for Teachers

Welcome to 'Success with GCSE Drama'. Let us begin by explaining the nativity of this book. As practising Drama teachers we have been annoyed and frustrated by the lack of any meaningful Drama book that could be used at KS4. Why is it that publishers seem to think that Drama means Theatre? That we want endless explanations about stagecraft and how to make a puppet? Our frustration led us to the door of Folens Publishers and a warm welcome from people who understood education and were willing to listen to our ideas. The materials in this book are ideas we have spent some years working out and developing. They are materials we have shared with a countless number of Drama teachers who have visited us throughout that time; and they always made the same point.

The lack of a formal programme of study and assessment framework has meant absolute flexibility, particularly at KS3. This means that when teaching at KS4, the demands of a GCSE specification has posed problems. How do you respond to the requirements of GCSE? We have created a programme of study that addresses both key stages. Our KS3 book – The Complete Guide to Successful Drama – provides a thorough framework for the teacher. This book builds on that framework and advances GCSE students through the same concepts. We have created four 'units' that build progression into a complete GCSE course. We have ensured the units are broad enough to be interpreted to meet any major Drama GCSE specification.

Finally, we should recognise the considerable support and advice we have been given by the many Drama teachers who have read and criticised the materials in this book. Their comments and suggestions have been invaluable, as has the advice provided by our friends at the University of Warwick. Last, but not least, we are indebted to our current Year 10 and 11 students who have offered ideas, thrown out ours and even taken part in photographing the illustrations for this book. They claim ownership of the idea for the DVD and won't accept we thought of it first!

The next four pages explain the principles of how the book works. Many of our colleagues have commented on the complexity of the basic concept at first glance. Yep – it is complex! But, we contend, so is Drama anyway! We believe we have provided:

- A relevant, GCSE-related programme of study that connects to each lesson's learning.

- Meaningful opportunities to use Assessment for Learning with students.

- A framework that is focused on independent learning that allows any student the opportunity to take responsibility for their learning.

Achieving these three essential goals is possible but requires a mindset that both teacher and student must embrace. It won't happen overnight but our experience proves that it will take shape very quickly. Our students are testimony to this fact.

We hope you find this book an asset in your curriculum planning. Ideally it will save you a lot of work or give you inspiration or ideas that will provoke your own responses. Whatever your thoughts, we'd be interested to know what you think.

You can contact us at **phil.parker@colmers.bham.sch.uk** or **craig.boardman@colmers.bham.sch.uk** – we look forward to hearing from you.

Introduction for Teachers

A Student-Friendly Drama Framework

It is our firmly held belief that an effective curriculum is one that must be understood by the students. If they cannot work independently within it or use its language to speak and write about it, then how can they succeed in it? It is for this reason we have taken the concepts, knowledge and skills of GCSE specifications and deconstructed them into a Drama Framework. We have simplified it so that it can be understood and used by KS3 students and built in progression so that it remains relevant to GCSE students. Continuity therefore happens from Year 7 through to Year 11. It works on the following premise:

1. Drama is frequently about telling a story. Its narrative form will vary, of course, but the basic tenet is that students of all ages gradually increase their sophistication in conveying a narrative to an audience. Hence the 'strand' – Narrative Structure.

2. Drama is equally about interpreting events through the eyes of another person. When performing a story, students engage in its telling through the character they play. We make them aware of that character's perspective and the factors that influence it. This is why we have the 'strand' of Character Development.

3. Relating a story from any character's perspective is done with an audience in mind. (To do otherwise suggests an introspective indulgence!) Interpreting events and feelings for an audience is the purpose of all art. How the audience may be influenced, the reactions students want to provoke, centres on our final strand – Audience Awareness.

What other subject can hand our young people the world and ask them to interpret what they find in order to provoke reaction from other people?

Each of the three 'strands' comprises components that help fulfil the title:

Narrative Structure	Character Development	Audience Awareness
Students will set out to achieve a specific intention for their drama based on the stimulus they have been given	When creating a character, students need to determine the sort of effect they want to have on their audience	In devising the drama, students need to decide what impact they want to provoke from their audience
Such stories are invariably built on some form of conflict and follow how characters may finally resolve such conflict	Characters, with any depth, need an arc that shows how they began the story and what changes happen to them as a result of events	Communicating to the audience can be done by their use of staging, which will include considering the pace of the piece
Students then need to learn how to plot a story in order to include relevant dramatic devices to achieve their intention	In communicating these characters to an audience, students need to consider the physical skills needed to achieve the planned effect	Inherent in any story is the tension needed to sustain the audience's interest, which builds to some form of climax

In creating such a Drama Framework, it is essential that its concepts and vocabulary are used equally by the students. These nine 'areas' prescribe the body of knowledge needed to fulfil any GCSE course. If they are to be used by students they should then be used as the basis for assessment also. Meaningful assessment should overlay the body of knowledge – or programme of study.

Introduction for Teachers

Student-Friendly Assessment within the Framework

'Perhaps assessment should be an activity done less to pupils and more with them?'

[Elizabeth Engel Clough, 1984]

This quotation has been our guide in the search for a meaningful Drama curriculum. Another source of influence has been the work of Paul Black explained in the Black Box series, from where we have taken this quotation:

> *The term 'assessment' refers to all those activities undertaken by teachers, and their students in assessing themselves, which provide information to be used as feedback to modify the teaching and learning activities in which they are engaged. Such assessment becomes 'formative assessment' when the evidence is actually used to adapt the teaching work to meet the needs.*

Our Drama Framework makes explicit what is to be learned so that teachers and students can both use it in order to identify how they – and their work – are progressing. Whilst we realise that GCSE criteria inevitably are needed for summative assessment, the Framework provides for formative and diagnostic assessment. We have built in three sessions to each unit that encourage students to review each other's work and help chart the response that informs further planning. We use peer assessment a lot, via the use of 'buddy groups'. They become familiar with the concepts and language of the Framework and use it to evaluate and review what their buddies perform. This means that students become familiar with the learning needed in GCSE Drama, in a way that simply sharing the GCSE criteria can never achieve. The Review and Respond pro-formas in each session provide a 'thinking frame' that encourages and structures this sort of evaluation.

Independent Learning within the Framework

With an explicit programme of study and an assessment system that reinforces it, students become utterly familiar with the whole Framework. It didn't take long to realise that students could use the Framework to such an extent that they became independent of us as teachers. Like all good systems, it is simple. It requires students to take responsibility for and lead in each of the three strands, like this:

Narrative Structure – is the domain of the students who we call Storytellers. Students with this role are responsible for leading their group in the devising and organisation of ideas that deliver their intention, where conflict is introduced and resolved and the structure of the drama has a clear plot that delivers the intention.

Character Development – is the strand belonging to Acting Coaches. These students help others in their group to determine the effect they want to create, provide ideas and feedback concerning the clarity of their character arc and their physical performance.

Audience Awareness – is managed by Directors. These students provide the objective feedback concerning how successfully the group is getting across their impact, and how well the staging and tension contributes to it.

This is why all the sessions are organised through these three roles. It ensures explicit coverage of the learning and offers regular and varied methods of evaluation of it. Our lessons offer a varied diet; sometimes a student will act as a Director in one lesson and become a Storyteller in the next. Other times they will remain as Director for the whole unit.

How to use this book

This book contains four units that can be developed into a GCSE scheme of work that will potentially cover the whole of KS4. Each unit is made up of:

- an introduction outlining the nature of what is to be learned

- six teaching sessions that lead students through a range of activities

- a script written especially for that unit that illustrates the learning.

We anticipate the units providing the progression needed in the order they appear – i.e., The Sophie Smithson Unit offers a simple introduction to the concepts needed in GCSE and we start Year 10 in this way. We finish Year 11 with The Choice – annually voted by students as the most successful scheme within our KS4 curriculum.

The Introductions

Each introduction contains a section for the *teacher* and the *student*; an outline of the learning in each session (called the Production Outline); any additional Support Material; a Narrative Menu (giving ideas for where the work might go once the six sessions are completed); Written Coursework ideas (which help support the theory requirements of all three major exam boards); and finally the Unit Review Frames which are photocopiable resources for your students to assess themselves on how much they've contributed to their group's work by the end of each unit.

The Sessions

- Each session is broken into three parts – Storytellers, Acting Coaches and Directors.

- At the top right hand side is the learning focus for each of these roles, (e.g. a Storyteller's page will have a box saying 'Narrative Structure' and INTENTION highlighted to show that the story's *intention* is being looked at in that session).

- Each page is then shaped by the following areas –
  - **'What you will learn'** explains the objectives for that session for the student.
  - **'What you need to know'** shows what previous knowledge and background will be needed to tackle the tasks presented in the session.
  - **'What you need to do'** takes the student through the main activity in that session.
  - **'Hints and Tips'** give support about how to achieve that activity.
  - **'How your group will help'** explains the activities of others in their group.
  - **'Example'** shows one possible way of tackling the activity.

- Session 2, of every unit, provides an opportunity for informal peer assessment.

- In Sessions 4 and 6 this assessment is more formally presented. The formal assessments (using 'buddies') can be photocopied and used by the students to reflect and review the work under scrutiny. This feedback is useful to each group in evaluating how effective their work is so far and where it might go in the future.

The Scripts

Each script runs for around 25 minutes and has five or six characters in it. They are written to support and illustrate the learning in that unit and can be used as a stimulus text for Edexcel or a performance text for AQA. Please feel free to alter character names or numbers and change or add any of the dialogue to suit your needs. These are presented to help you, so please use them to that effect.

Introduction for Teachers

The DVD

As an additional teaching resource, we have included samples of some of our students illustrating aspects of each unit. Their performances are taken from each of the scripts, and include their discussions as Storytellers, Directors and Acting Coaches as they work on these texts. A complete performance of 'The Choice' script shows *their* interpretation. We are sure this resource can be used in many ways, not least as a stimulus to discussion.

Frequently Asked Questions

Q: Why do we need to have Storytellers, Directors and Acting Coaches?

A: By focusing the responsibilities for their learning, students are able to take ownership of specific parts of group work. The definition of the three roles ensures ALL areas of ANY GCSE course are covered within the teaching and learning. Our experience tells us that, *once established*, it leads to **personalised learning**. Students know what is to be achieved and identify the best ways to achieve it. It is a truly *shared* curriculum. We recommend students take turns in assuming each responsibility.

Q: How, as a teacher, can I keep track of what is being taught and learned?

A: The 'drop down menus' in the top, right corner of each session show which part of the curriculum is being covered for a particular learner. Learning objectives and the activities are all linked into it, so you can see, at a glance, what is being covered.

Q: How does assessment work in this framework?

A: All GCSE specifications require students to be reflective in their work. The assessments *encourage and structure* this reflection. 'Buddies' provide objective feedback against previously specified objectives and students then consider what amendments are needed in their work as a result. Each student is assessed within their area of responsibility, (e.g. other Directors in the class give evaluative feedback to the Director being assessed).

Q: What form does this assessment process take?

A: Firstly, the assessed 'strand' (e.g. 'impact' for Directors) will have something new introduced *during the previous sessions* that can be used to good effect within the assessment in Sessions 2, 4 and 6.

The Unit Review Frames provide each student with a chance to record *how* they have achieved each of the objectives set out in their assessments by the *end of the unit*. It holds them *accountable* for their learning, helping individualised target setting.

Q: Is this supposed to replace the GCSE assessments?

A: Not at all. They are 'summative' assessments. Our process is 'formative' assessment – designed to give feedback and aid future planning. Buddies provide the feedback; the student's future planning is better informed by such feedback. This process encourages structured reflection and planning – a key part of all GCSE assessment.

Introduction for Students

Welcome to 'Success with GCSE Drama'. We hope this book will form part of your Drama course that ensures you the best result you can achieve!

The main thing you need to understand about how this book works is that in each session, you are all going to have a particular part to play in achieving success in that session. You will take responsibility for the leadership of one of these three jobs:

STORYTELLER (S)

Responsible for the Narrative Structure of the drama – making sure the story is told in a way that captures the interest of your audience and gets across a message to them too. This means you will need to:

- Lead the group in planning the intention for the drama, making sure your discussion will lead to the creation of an Overall Objective and also develop ideas that will help to achieve it.
- Chair discussions that are geared to working out the purpose of each part of your story and the reactions you want to provoke from the audience.
- Make sure the group considers how the motives of key characters will affect the storyline, getting them to think of ways that such motives will drive the story.
- Lead the development of the structure of the drama, making sure it has a clear beginning, middle and end.
- Encourage your group to find ways to 'hook' the audience into any conflict and so make the audience care about what happens to the characters in the story.
- Lead the search for a satisfying, dramatic climax to the drama.
- Make sure the group always keep their attention focused upon 'the big picture' – through the Overall Objective – rather than on minor details all the time. They can leave the minor details to the Director.

ACTING COACH (C)

Responsible for Character Development in the drama – working to improve the quality of the way your group plays the characters. This means you will need to:

- Assist actors in the creation of characterisations which fit the needs of the piece, thereby helping to achieve your Overall Objective.
- Assist actors in discussing the sort of effect they aim to achieve and identify the sort of actions and words that are needed to achieve that goal.
- Give feedback to actors on how well they provoke reactions from the audience and what sequences of words and actions might help to reach this goal.
- Give accurate feedback to actors as they try to use their physical skills such as voice, facial expressions, gestures, body language and movement.
- Assess how well motivation is conveyed to the audience, how clear it is and how it links to the Overall Objective. To give suggestions where needed.
- Suggest ideas about characters' backgrounds and how a character arc can be created and shown to the audience in order to give a characterisation depth. Make sure the character has changed in some way by the end of the drama.

D **DIRECTOR**

Responsible for the Audience Awareness in the drama – to provide your group with the audience's viewpoint and give feedback about how they might react – and why.
This means you will need to:

- Make sure you direct your group in 'marking the moments' so they perform in such a way that makes clear your Overall Objective to the audience.
- Lead your group to identify the intended impact you want to have on your audience and suggest ways it can be achieved.
- Find ways that your drama connects with your audience, so they can relate to it, and resonates with them.
- Emphasise the use of space by thinking about your staging, so that it can convey signals to the audience, signals regarding status, relationships and tension.
- Explain to the audience the time, atmosphere and location of your drama.
- Check the use of pace to keep your audience involved and able to follow what is happening, understanding that pace needs to vary in good drama.
- Direct your actors using techniques that create or develop tension.
- Make sure the right balance is maintained between providing the audience with exposition (so they understand what is happening, and why) and providing the tension that keeps their attention and interest.

What do you need to do?

You will want to take on each of these three responsibilities as you work through these units. Each area will help you become successful Drama students BUT one thing to bear in mind:

In order to be a good Leader you must first become a good Listener.

When you take on one of these roles, you will need to cooperate with others in your group, listen to their ideas and try to meet them half way when arguments happen. Not to do this will mean people won't follow you! You will learn a great deal about leadership and responsibility by working in this way. With the right amount of such leadership and cooperation it will mean that, as a group, you will be able to create great dramas!

Everyone will have a part to play – not just as a character in the story – but also by knowing what it is they will need to do to make the drama great!

What will you learn from this book?

In the Introduction to this book we have explained that Drama can be divided into three areas. These are – ways of telling a story, creating and developing a character and always having the audience in mind.

Listed below are all the things you will learn from the four units within this book.

Narrative Structure (Telling Stories)

Unit 1: Sophie Smithson

Your intention is what you want to perform from the stimulus you are given

The issues you explore can become your theme, once you have decided what you want to say about those issues

Your intention for a scene is what you always keep in mind when choosing your ideas

Conflict occurs when characters have different motives

Conflict needs to be 'mapped' throughout the story, so it crops up at key moments

An Overall Objective – the goal your group sets that affects all your storytelling decisions

Unit 2: Modern Tales

The emotional response from your audience needs to be built into the story structure

Creating openings and endings that get across your theme and reinforce the Overall Objective

Any story needs to build 'steps' towards a definite climax; this is the plot

Character Development (Creating Characters)

Unit 1: Sophie Smithson

An effect is when your character provokes reactions from the audience

Character motivation helps to create a specific emotional effect on the audience

Your theme helps you identify the character 'types' you need to develop for your drama

Characters show depth when they have a past that is shown, which creates a character arc

Different emotions can cause conflict which can affect motivations, creating an arc

An Overall Objective – the goal your group sets that affects all your character choices

Unit 2: Modern Tales

Avoid playing stereotypes by getting across motivation clearly to the audience

'Flashbacks' are excellent ways to show a character's past, that helps create an arc

Physical skills used by the actor can signal to the audience aspects of the characterisation

Audience Awareness (Considering the Audience)

Unit 1: Sophie Smithson

The theme of your drama needs to impact upon your audience, provoking feelings from them

Status shows who has authority and power in a scene and can be shown by high/low positions on stage

'Marking the moment' draws the audience's attention to a specific important event

Staging helps to comment on relationships by the space between characters

The space onstage (staging) shows the conflict between characters, creating tension

An Overall Objective – the goal your group sets that affects all your directing decisions

Unit 2: Modern Tales

Status can provoke emotional reactions from the audience such as sympathy and hatred

Staging helps you convey ideas about communication by the way space is used onstage

Tension needs to be built up in 'steps' in order to create a climax in a drama

What will you learn from this book?

Unit 3: Shadowfall

'Hooking' your audience helps your intention by making the audience want to see more of the story

'Exposition' is when you explain to the audience what is happening and why

'Flashbacks' are a useful storytelling tool that explain part of the plot, giving essential information to the audience

Showing your theme needs to be done not only by words but by actions also

Conflict can be created by a moral dilemma for a character, an internal conflict

Unit 3: Shadowfall

Physical skills used by the actor sometimes replace the need for speech

Reactions between characters show their relationship when words are not available

Physical skills can show how a character has changed over a period of time, giving depth to our belief in them

Characters' reactions need to be realistic, otherwise the audience won't believe in what they do

Any character arc needs to have a range of emotions for that character to show an audience

Unit 3: Shadowfall

To create an impact on your audience you need to 'hook' them at the start

Clever staging keeps a scene 'alive' when there is a lot of speech to be delivered

'Flashbacks' help explain present situations but it must be obvious to the audience it is a different time or location

Contrast is a good way to show tension, by varying the speed of a scene – what we call 'pace'

'Emotional tension' is when you direct a scene to make the audience care for the characters

Unit 4: The Choice

'Resonance' is when the audience 'connect' with a character's experiences onstage

Conflicting motives for characters create tension for the audience

'Non-naturalistic' methods can be used to show any character's background for the audience

A 'montage' helps convey moods to the audience

It is important that the audience understand a character if they are to sympathise with them – so their actions must be explained

The ending of a play needs to capture the mood of the theme

Unit 4: The Choice

Characters in a drama need to contrast, thereby helping create your planned effect

Physical skills of the actor can help build tension by their reactions

'Non-naturalistic' methods can get the audience inside the mind of a character

A 'montage' helps convey several sides to a character

Physical skills can be used to show a character's decision, it isn't always necessary to use words

Characters' emotions should be shown in a subtle way – not always 'over the top' – remember 'less is more'

Unit 4: The Choice

Contrasting emotions can help improve the impact you have on your audience

Tension onstage is helped by 'rhythm', when the speed of events change in a scene/play

'Non-naturalistic' staging can be effective when showing characters' thoughts/feelings

A 'montage' can help show the passage of time to the audience

'Cross-cutting' changes the traditional way of performing a scene and creates a dramatic way of staging it

Contrast is important at the ending of a play, an emotional climax is emphasised by a quiet ending

What will you learn from this book?

Having shown you what is being taught in this book, let us now explain what you should be able to show in your drama.

In NARRATIVE STRUCTURE (Storytelling)

If you understand the **INTENTION** of the story then you will achieve this:

Your intention has been communicated! The performance leaves no doubt at all what is being said. The purpose is very clear. The story moves from beginning to end with clear reasons explained as to how we get there. The story sets out to get across a message and succeeds. Each scene has a reason for being there and they are linked together by the Overall Objective. Each actor in the story has a role to play in getting across this message to the audience and clearly 'does their bit' successfully.

If you understand the **CONFLICT** in the story then you will achieve this:

You have chosen an exciting story! The drama progresses with suspense shown at every turn!
The conflict arises out of the motivations of the characters and is completely believable for this reason. Effective staging is used to emphasise the conflict and a range of physical techniques (voice, etc.) complement it. The conflict is built effectively to a good climax. However, the prime factor is that the conflict is one that arises out of the theme and message – showing the dilemma characters face and the different sides of the dilemma provoke the conflict.

If you understand the **PLOT** in the story then you will achieve this:

You take the audience on a real journey. The story develops very clearly and with genuine belief because the actions are always linked to characters' motives. These motives are always communicated to the audience by clever use of dialogue and actions – in such a way it's not obvious it is happening. The story has a clear beginning, a middle and a strong end that leaves the audience satisfied that everything has been 'tied up neatly' – not only explained but also it seems the right things have happened and we can believe them.

In CHARACTER DEVELOPMENT

If you understand the **EFFECT** you want to develop then you will achieve this:

An emotional success for the actor! The audience is moved emotionally, perhaps to hate or to cry in sympathy. The point is that the actor has chosen to play, and successfully achieved, a characterisation that has had a profound effect – the audience reacts strongly! The character links with the group's Overall Objective clearly and the impact they intended to have has been achieved through this character.

If you understand the **CHARACTER ARC** you want to develop then you will achieve this:

The actor has mapped an exciting characterisation that has a clear background which moves through relevant motives to end in a complete and well understood arc. It is clear that this character's motives have changed throughout the story and they are now a different character and that is clear to the audience. The reason for them changing is credible. Also, the actor has planned how this will happen, with carefully worked-out speeches that explain everything to the audience. It is like we can draw a continuous line from the story's start to the end for this character.

If you understand the **PHYSICAL** skills you want to develop then you will achieve this:

Physically, the performer plays a character thoroughly unlike their own self. Clever use of movement, body language, voice and face has meant an utterly believable characterisation. It has been well coordinated with the intended 'effect' the performer set out to achieve, even down to minute detail, such as mannerisms, gestures and voice. The voice has been used effectively with excellent diction, good projection and volume. Physically there are occasions when the actor has clearly linked physical actions with key words in their speeches. Excellent control is used throughout.

What will you learn from this book?

In AUDIENCE AWARENESS

If you understand the **IMPACT** you want to develop then you will achieve this:

> The drama will stir the audience's emotions, provoking the response chosen. The emotions stirred have been a direct result of the narrative and the characterisations chosen. This response has been carefully planned, using clever use of script, staging, character, relationships and mood. This high level of impact has been well sustained throughout the drama, leaving the audience drained! There is clear evidence of well-planned ideas being chosen that significantly achieve the emotional destination aimed for.

If you understand the **STAGING** you want to develop then you will achieve this:

> The staging of this piece of drama clearly and effectively gets across the intended impact/message. Space has been used clearly to convey status/tension/relationships. It has been used effectively, because of the way the stage becomes a tool to get across the message/impact of the piece. Inventive ways have been mapped to achieve this goal which draws the audience's attention to the staging for this purpose.

If you understand the **TENSION** you want to develop then you will see this:

> A gripping piece! The drama has provoked real excitement and suspense! A range of techniques to create tension – and sustain it – have been used. (Examples such as pauses, looks between characters, keeping the action speedy, etc.) We have been left wondering what is going to happen next on lots of occasions. The audience has been focused on the events in case they miss something. Clever planning has meant key moments that add to the tension, like steps, and have been well thought out, building to a great climax! A varied pace has been deliberately planned in order to build to this climax.

How will I know how I am doing?

A major part of doing well in GCSE Drama is being able to *reflect* on the work you are creating. We have made Session 4 and Session 6 into 'mini-assessments' for this reason. As Storytellers, Acting Coaches and Directors, you will be given particular goals to achieve, based on what you have been taught recently. It will be your task to show you understand what you have been taught and that you can use that knowledge.

Buddies can help!

We've suggested that you use 'buddies' to help show you how well you are doing. For example, if you are a Director trying to create 'impact' in your assessment, we suggest other Directors (who are doing the same task) give you feedback about how well you are doing in achieving your goals after they've seen your scene performed. This will give you a chance to *reflect and plan* where you go next with your directing for 'impact'. You can help another Director in the same way. The result should be a sharper, better quality and clearer piece of work that will get you better marks hopefully!

The Five-Step Assessment Process

Step 1: You are given your stimulus or setting

We give you information about the scene you are going to help create. We might give you a situation or important information that causes you to react.

What will you learn from this book?

Step 2: Decide what role you are going to take

This means deciding, firstly, if you are going to be assessed as a Storyteller, Acting Coach or Director. (This may depend on the role you have been taking in previous sessions.) Whichever role you take, you will see you are given *more* information about the work you are going to create on the first page of the assessment sessions. Look at the responsibilities listed on pages 10–11 to help you realise what you will need to do.

Step 3: Make sure you know and understand your 'goals' for the assessment

On the second page of the assessment session you will see you are given precise 'goals' to achieve as a Storyteller, Acting Coach or Director. These goals are how you will be assessed. Can you successfully make sure all of them are achieved? They are all connected to whatever you are being assessed on. Keep them uppermost in your thoughts at all times! Your success depends on it.

Step 4: Getting feedback on your goals

Having worked out what the scene will be like with your group, you now perform it to another group – your 'buddies'. They will assess how well you are doing like this:

- 'Buddies' are people doing the same job as you. They will assess you against the same goals that *they* have.
- They will watch the scene to see if they can find evidence of your involvement in achieving your goals.
- They will give you feedback by ticking boxes on the third page and answer questions about what they have seen using the goals as their guide.
- Once they have done that, you will do the same for them.

Step 5: Planning what you do next

Now your buddies have given you their feedback, you need to think what you should do with that advice. What are the concerns you have been shown by your buddy? Again, there are boxes to tick on the fourth and last page to answer this. What improvements can you make? There are also explanation boxes for you to complete in more detail, which helps you plan what you must look at next.

For it is now your job to find solutions for those concerns in order to lead your group in improving the *quality* of your scene *even further*!

End of Unit Reviews

Once you have completed *all* your assessments, after Session 6, you need to review your achievements personally. The Unit Review Frame found in each unit will help you reflect on what *you* have done. If you have been a Storyteller you will find all the goals you have been given as a Storyteller in this unit. It will be up to you to find *evidence* to show how you achieved those goals. This is a great way for you to reflect on what you have actually learned in this unit.

There is also a section for you set yourself a target for next time you take on that role. You can identify an area for which you may not have enough evidence or an aspect you may not have understood quite as well. The information on pages 14–15 may help you here.

This activity will help you review and reflect on your work, your ideas and your learning. It is only by constantly reflecting on these things that you improve. If you use this process wisely and productively you will be able to progress in Drama! Good luck!

The Sophie Smithson Investigation

Synopsis

A police inspector arrives at a youth club investigating the death of a 15-year-old girl. Though no one has actually killed her, several of the teenagers are shown to be responsible for the events leading to her death. She was an orphan; poor and lonely. That was enough to make her different. Enough to make her a target. A victim. Then it turns out she isn't dead. Until another police inspector arrives…

This is a modern-day version of J.B.Priestley's *'An Inspector Calls'*. Like Priestley's play, this drama looks at the issues of peer pressure and social responsibility. It follows the gang responsible for tormenting this poor girl and how, eventually, the events affect all of them in turn…

Sophie Smithson Unit Outline

SESSION FLOWCHART

S STORYTELLER

Session 1
Creating an intention that makes the audience think about peer pressure

Session 2
Producing the right context for peer pressure as a theme

Session 3
Understand that conflict arises from characters' motives

Session 4
Develop a message for the drama about social responsibility

Session 5
Understand conflict causes tension

Session 6
Plotting a scene that meets the Overall Objective

C ACTING COACH

Session 1
Creating an effect that defines the characters

Session 2
Creating possible characters to play and show motives

Session 3
Understand how to use the past to create a character arc

Session 4
Develop a message for the drama about social responsibility

Session 5
Creating characters that produce tension

Session 6
Using physical skills to convey both character and tension

D DIRECTOR

Session 1
Establishing the impact, creating sympathy and dislike

Session 2
Improving the impact to enhance the theme

Session 3
Using staging to show isolation of a character

Session 4
Develop a message for the drama about social responsibility

Session 5
Understand conflict causes tension

Session 6
Directing a scene that meets the Overall Objective

Teacher-in-Role (Session 3)

One of the major factors that make this unit popular is the role of Detective Inspector Goole. We play this character with a sharp-tongued ruthlessness and hostility. This is a character who doesn't take prisoners. This officer tells students of Sophie Smithson's suicide after drinking disinfectant. This heightened emotional stance provokes heightened and varied reactions! It is a role which makes some students' characters react with the same hostility, others capitulate under the torrent of questioning – which is the intention of this character.

We set up the Youth Club scene deliberately and spend time establishing its context with descriptions of police officers outside the door, blue lights flashing on cars. We build the tension that arises out of the unknown suddenly appearing on their doorstep.

After acting out this meeting with D.I. Goole, we evaluate their reactions.

We normally conduct some simple improvisations that look at the reactions of the characters a few hours later.

Then… We deliberately re-establish the Youth Club setting again. We emphasise that 24 hours have elapsed. They are back in the Youth Club and again the police have arrived. They expect more interrogation by the ruthless D.I. Goole. However, this time it is another police officer. Again, they are told of Sophie's death – but this time in a road traffic accident that has just taken place as she ran out of the Youth Club. Déjà vu it seems?

We play the second officer very differently to emphasise the difference with the first meeting. This officer is soft-spoken, polite and sympathetic and unaware of the first officer who isn't known to their force.

In the evaluations of this second session we usually arrive at the ghostly ('Goole') police officer being the 'gang's' conscience – as is the case with the J.B. Priestley character – from where we adapted the idea.

This session – though quite often lengthy – does provide a strong stimulus that students enjoy. It provides a clear focus for the thematic introduction of social responsibility. However, the unit works well on its own without you having to introduce this supernatural element, if you feel your students would benefit from a simpler story.

Coursework Opportunities

This unit provides materials that will meet coursework requirements for the main exam boards. Several options are provided for extended writing as well as the formal Paper 1 Response stipulated by AQA. We have not cluttered the sessions with suggestions but rather left the choices up to the teacher in this introductory section.

Assessment for Learning

From our experiences of using Assessment for Learning in our lessons, we have built in assessments that focus upon explicit elements of our Assessment and Curriculum Framework. Some teachers may not want to use the assessment aspect of Sessions 2, 4 and 6. We contend that this would be a waste. We get our groups to choose a 'buddy group' who they regularly share their ideas with and perform to. These sessions merely formalise this practice, in the assumption it gives the group objective feedback that allows them to review others' work and project their own responses based upon their feedback.

Sophie Smithson Unit Outline

Sophie Smithson Unit Outline

Students' Outline of this Unit

You've all seen it happen: at school, on the bus, at youth club, passing in the street. That person who doesn't quite fit in with everyone else? You've seen how they are treated; called names, jokes are made about them, sworn at maybe? Perhaps you've been a part of that treatment. Perhaps you've been the victim?

This story is about such treatment, about such attitudes. Sophie Smithson is 15 years old. She is an orphan who lives in a children's home. She hasn't got very much money. She hasn't got people to buy her fashionable clothes. So she's isolated.

Like the law of the jungle, the lonely and the weak are the ones who are attacked. So it is with Sophie. After particularly harsh treatment by a gang at Youth Club she takes her life. This provokes an investigation by a ruthless and unpleasant police officer.

Now all the gang is put under the microscope, their treatment of Sophie analysed. Because someone is guilty of driving her to her death...!

(S) STORYTELLER

As Storyteller you will lead the search for ideas – ways of showing:

- how peer pressure works, why we do it when we know it's wrong
- how people can suffer from it and what the consequences are
- why so many people end up being vindictive, spiteful and cruel.

You will also lead the decision-making in choosing the structure of your drama:

- deciding what conflict should be included and what causes it
- deciding how the dramatic climax of the story should be shaped
- deciding how the message of social responsibility will be shown in the drama.

(C) ACTING COACH

As Acting Coach you will lead in defining and developing characters so:

- these characters are explained by their motives, whatever drives them
- the behaviour they show arises out of these motives
- characters 'mark the moment' which shows who they are to the audience.

You will lead the decision-making in improving the quality of characterisations by:

- getting actors to think of showing their backgrounds and relationships to others
- developing physical skills, like voice and movement, to convey their character
- finding situations that allow characterisations to be seen at their best so that the actor can directly affect how they are seen by the audience.

(D) DIRECTOR

As Director you will take the lead in focusing the audience's attention on:

- what the downside of peer pressure is, what harm it causes
- how people are pressured into doing things they know to be wrong
- how people react when they are found guilty of such negative pressure.

You will lead the decision-making in establishing the tone, pace and staging so that:

- staging can be used effectively to show the conflict within the story
- the audience experience the feelings of those who suffer, creating real impact
- the climax is made effective by setting the right tone by the use of pace.

Production Outline

Session 1
A scene at a party where Sophie (whom we don't ever see) is wearing old-fashioned clothes. It makes her look odd and out of place. This scene focuses upon the reactions of the characters onstage, how people are pressurised to do spiteful things and what motives they have for doing so, which makes us dislike them.

Session 2
A scene in a classroom after Sophie Smithson has left. Some of the characters in a gang are jealous of her academic success. They decide to play spiteful tricks. This scene focuses upon characters pressurising others which makes us angry at them, as well as deciding the motives of specific characters in the gang.

Session 3
The spiteful pranks directed at Sophie, this time even more hurtful and vindictive than before. Now, though, one of the boys in the gang suffers just as much. The nature of this prank is so malicious; it prompts some of the other gang members to come into conflict with the gang leader and bully. The boy concerned becomes isolated, as the gang must decide whether they stand by their friend or submit to the pressure of the leader.

Session 4
After being visited by a ruthless and unpleasant police officer 'the gang' are left to react to the news. Some are afraid, anxious that their actions could have consequences that involve the police. Others are less afraid but realise, if they are to remain safe, that they must make sure the 'weaker' ones don't get them into trouble. Now we see the darker side of peer pressure and how it can overcome our usual social responsibility to one another.

Session 5
The need to confess grows with some of the gang; they are now the victims – of their own feelings of guilt. Outside the police station a situation arises that tears the gang apart. We look at staging here, especially, as we see the 'ebb and flow' of power in the gang.

Session 6
The climax of the story. Sick of being pressured to do things they know to be wrong, some of the gang stand up to the bullies. This scene looks at how and why the 'balance of power' gradually shifts – away from the bullies and towards the others. It allows us to get our message across to the audience. We look at how status can help us here, as well as tension techniques. The physical performance of characters is also covered here.

And so the story goes on… Ideas are then provided about how you can create your own drama from this material using what you've learned and been encouraged to think about.

The following extracts are part of a diary found, torn up, in Sophie Smithson's room at The Oaks children's home.

SATURDAY

It was so embarrassing. I had saved up the money for weeks to buy the dress. I had hoped someone might come shopping with me, but, of course, they all had better things to do. I couldn't afford the fashionable shops, just didn't have enough money! So I hoped no one would see me coming out of the shop I eventually bought the dress from. Just my luck, there she was! With her grinning little friend, laughing at me, making fun of what I'd bought. I thought the stripes had made me look slim. Of course she says that I look like a human peppermint in the dress! I'll never be able to wear it now! And it'll be round school on Monday. WHY CAN'T I EVER GET ANYTHING RIGHT?

MONDAY

The English results came out today. Awful news! I came top! Why couldn't I just have not tried and then I wouldn't have done so well and wouldn't have got noticed! Everyone just stared at me when the teacher read out the results. Why did he have to read them out? Why not just put the marks in our books then people might never know!

Of course, now she is annoyed with me. Little Miss I'm-Always-Brilliant-at-English. Except now I've arrived, I seem to have taken the title from her. She's going to be jealous and resentful of me now and that means I'll suffer. She and her friends will make my life hell now. Why have I got to be clever?

TUESDAY

I don't normally eat in the dining room at school. Can't afford their prices for one thing but also it really looks bad when you have no one to sit with. I couldn't understand why the table by the window wasn't being used. Should have known I'd do something wrong, it's all I ever do! This bully comes along and says it's theirs and knocks my food on to the floor. The teacher on duty ends up believing the bully not me and makes me pick it all up! Life is so unfair! What have I done to deserve this?

WEDNESDAY

The event in the dining room yesterday has everyone looking and pointing at me, making jokes and calling me names. And I mean everyone! Even little kids are doing it! It's like something out of those nature programmes on TV. The weak animal is the one all the others attack – until it dies. And I'm the weakest animal in this jungle!

THURSDAY

I can't believe it! I mean, I've fancied him for ages. He's got a lovely smile and he seems really kind. I thought he would already be going out with someone else but he's asked me out to Youth Club. He must be really brave though! Everyone will give him a hard time because he's with me. Perhaps I should warn him? But I want to be with him! I've never had anyone show me kindness before. Perhaps, just for a little while, I could have someone be nice towards me? Just once?

Sophie Smithson Scheme Outline

You may want to consider using some of these scenes in your interpretation (after Session 6).

OPTION 1

Story In a classroom, the gang have just humiliated Sophie, who's left. Some find it funny; others start to feel they've gone too far. They find her schoolbag; in it is a birthday card. Its Sophie's and today is her birthday. And look how they've just treated her!

Characters All the gang.

Storyteller Where does tension appear in this scene? Is there a climax at its end, brought about by different attitudes towards Sophie?

Acting Coach Who has the motive to speak up for Sophie? Who has the courage to 'be different' in front of the gang?

Director Are cracks in the gang's loyalty showing here? Some may disagree how far to go to pick on Sophie. How do you 'mark the moment' to show this?

OPTION 2

Story One of the gang has been seen talking to Sophie on their own. There are accusations made about this person and their relationship with Sophie that illustrates how peer pressure works – you can't be seen with an 'outcast'!

Characters All the gang.

Storyteller The scene only ever has two people at a time, as one leaves another enters and the story is passed on rather like Chinese whispers. Perhaps it ends with the first person to leave entering again, hearing a different story from what they first told!

Acting Coach A chance to see characters' relationships with each other.

Director This scene can be quite funny as the story changes each time. There is a serious message behind it, so how can the tone at the end of the scene show this serious message?

OPTION 3

Story The Police Station. One of the gang has unexpectedly been interviewed, so the others want to know what has been said – and to find out if they are in trouble, or next up to be interviewed.

Characters All the gang.

Storyteller There will be suspicion and a lack of trust here. How can you show this?

Acting Coach Why do they not trust each other? Is it because some of them don't feel as responsible as others? Will they want to take any blame therefore?

Director Should we feel sorry for any of these characters? Or do they all deserve any trouble that comes their way? How can you 'mark the moment' that illustrates this? A moment where we see someone struggle emotionally? Or a moment where someone confronts their guilt?

OPTION 4

Story One of the gang has been persuaded to go out with Sophie, who has agreed to meet him at Youth Club. He has to dump her in public. A form of nasty ritual humiliation.

Characters All the gang.

Storyteller It would be nicely ironic if the boy concerned actually did like Sophie and so is reluctant to do this! How can this be shown however? He wouldn't admit to these feelings!

Acting Coach How can these two sides of the boy's feelings be shown? Does he have a friend he can confide in? Is the friend trustworthy?

Director How do you show the torment of the boy? You may need to stage this scene with the boy off to one side, so that his reactions are not seen by the others. This allows you to have him face the gang and turn away from them.

Sophie Smithson Unit Outline

Sophie Smithson Unit Outline

OPTION 5

Story Sophie's funeral. The gang attend, though possibly after everyone else has gone? It is a chance for some in the gang to show remorse as well as to place the blame for her death.

Characters All the gang.

Storyteller The tone of this scene is important. Funerals are quiet and respectful. This would be heightened by a noisy, argumentative outburst in the middle of the scene, to become quiet again at the end.

Acting Coach Who provokes the argument? Who is hurting the most at this point? Why do they hurt? Is it the boy mentioned in Option 4?

Director The tone referred to in the Storyteller section – involves a slowing down of the pace. Pauses between speeches for facial expressions, eye contact, changed positions on stage?

OPTION 6

Story The playground, Monday. Two of the gang have seen Sophie buying a really old-fashioned skirt and top from an unfashionable shop. They tell the others and use it as a chance to have a laugh at Sophie's expense. Perhaps one of the gang feels uncomfortable about this?

Characters All the gang.

Storyteller Get people entering one after another so each time the story is told, it is exaggerated and made funny!

Acting Coach Perhaps the girls are bitchy, the boys run Sophie down. But what are their motives for behaving this way? Motives must differ for each person, remember.

Director Find a way to make the audience laugh at the situation and then suddenly turn it round and inject a dramatic event at the end. This heightens the drama.

OPTION 7

Story Sophie's room at The Oaks Children's Home. She is having a nightmare. We don't see Sophie, just her bed. This could be a non-naturalistic scene to gain real impact.

Characters All the gang.

Storyteller Perhaps she sees the gang as the monsters that young children often believe live under the bed! So this is how they come to torment her!

Acting Coach Work with your actors on their movement here – to walk, slither or whatever – as monsters. How can they use their voices to sound monstrous? Are words used or sounds?

Director The purpose of this scene has to be to get the audience to appreciate Sophie's nightmare. Is this a chance to involve your audience in it? Perhaps the actors go into the audience? Could masks help achieve this effect?

OPTION 8

Story The inquest, the legal event that decides what caused Sophie's death. To create impact perhaps this is done in a non-naturalistic way? Legal voices heard offstage with silent action onstage.

Characters All the gang.

Storyteller A silent sequence onstage that involves actors using props. For example, as her parents' deaths are explained (offstage), a character picks up a teddy, looks sadly at it and then punches it, and drops it on the floor.

Acting Coach Coach your actors in the very formal way legal proceedings are spoken. Try to include some legal-sounding words.

Director Sympathy for Sophie must drive this scene. Props help here – what belongings might she have that have a story behind them? How might they be linked to the gang?

Written Coursework

Option 1

Write your own script for the events that happen in Session 6 – the climax of the Sophie Smithson story.

- Consider the elements to be addressed by Storytellers especially but also Directors and Acting Coaches – in order to get the characterisations right.
- Secondly you need to remember that scripts are mainly what the characters say. Therefore you must do all your explaining (your message, characters' motives, etc.) in the lines spoken by the actors.
- Try to make your script 'punchy' – keep the words to a minimum so that they have impact but make sure explanations of motives, settings, characters, etc. are given too.
- Use the 'plot' ideas earlier in this book as a checklist for the points to bear in mind when writing a script.

Option 2

Write a 'Response' – as in AQA's GCSE Drama Part 1.

This exercise involves you comparing the ideas you have for your drama with the work of another creator of good drama! We suggest comparing your work with that of J.B. Priestley who wrote a play called 'An Inspector Calls'.

The plot: This play, written in 1945, also deals with the theme of social responsibility. In this play the wealthy and smug Birling family are visited by a police inspector. He shows them, during the course of the play, that each one of them is responsible for the suicide of a young woman, Eva Smith. Eva is our version of Sophie Smithson. The family are shocked when, at the end and after the police inspector has left, the police station phone to tell them of the death that has just happened and that no police officer has been sent to see them – yet!

Themes: 'An Inspector Calls' is what is known as a 'well made play'. It moves from the characters and audience being in a position of not understanding something to eventually realising a truth. This is what we have suggested *you* need to do in your drama. The climax provides the message, when the inspector declares to the family that everyone is responsible for everyone else, we do not just look after ourselves. A fitting moral for a society just at the end of a World War! It is a moral that may well fit our society in the early twenty-first century.

Characters: The Birling family have numerous characters that you could compare with your work and from whom you could get ideas. The 'peer pressure' in this play is caused by people feeling they were rich enough not to care about others. The causes may have changed but the results of such pressure haven't. The victims still suffer.

Option 3

Create a series of diary entries (like we did for Sophie) that show your own 'character arc'. You can show what your character is like before the drama starts and then how the character develops over each of the events in each session. It may then help to identify what that character would do next. What might happen to them? How are they affected by what has happened? How can your diary entries convey the theme of social responsibility in what you have to say?

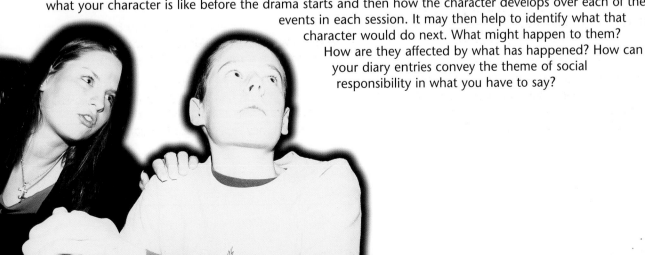

Unit Review Frame – Storyteller

S Name _____ Class _____ Date _____

*In this unit I have been responsible for leading my group in developing the **Narrative Structure** of our drama. This has meant working on getting ideas that help tell the story in such a way that it got across our thoughts about peer pressure and social responsibility. I have learned:*

INTENTION: *(when you set out to create a story/drama with a message)*

1. (Session 1) I was able to show how peer pressure works. I did this by:

2. (Session 2) I was able to show how people can suffer as a result of peer pressure. One of the ideas I organised, with my group's help, to show this was:

CONFLICT: *(showing differences in opinion/motives and how that affects the narrative)*

3. (Session 4) I helped show conflict arising from different motives by:

PLOT: *(how you structure or shape a drama to make a point)*

4. (Session 6) In order to create a climax to the drama we needed to create 'steps'. This taught me:

5. (Session 6) The climax of the drama is where the message is shown best. I realised this when:

Next time I take on the Storyteller role my target is:

Unit Review Frame – Acting Coach

C Name _____ Class _____ Date _____

*In this unit I have been responsible for leading my group in **Character Development** for our drama. This has meant helping the actors in my group to develop characters that comment on or reflect peer pressure and social responsibility. I have learned:*

EFFECT: *(when you set out to affect how and why the audience sees the character)*

1. (Session 1) I helped my group develop their characters' motives. I did this by:

2. (Session 2) I helped my group develop characters that pressured people. I did this by:

ARC: *(showing the growth of a character, from before the story to its climax)*

3. (Session 3) I helped my group show character arcs. I did this by:

PHYSICAL: *(the skills you use to communicate your character to the audience)*

4. (Session 6) You need motives to explain why your character does things. I learned:

5. (Session 6) I helped my group convey these motives physically by:

Next time I take on the Acting Coach role my target is:

Unit Review Frame **Acting Coach**

Unit Review Frame – Director

(D) **Name** ------------------------------------- **Class** -------------- **Date** --------------

*In this unit I have been responsible for leading my group in developing **Audience Awareness** in our drama. This has meant working on getting our message about peer pressure and social responsibility across to the audience clearly. I have learned:*

IMPACT: *[where you set out how your want your audience to react]*

1. (Session 1) I set out to make the audience feel angry about the characters at the party by:

2. (Session 2) I drew attention to characters suffering peer pressure by:

STAGING: *(using the space onstage to communicate with the audience)*

3. (Session 3) I used staging to show isolation onstage by:

TENSION: *(creating situations that make your audience wonder what will happen next)*

4. (Session 6) I have learned to draw attention to key events, 'marking the moment' by:

5. (Session 6) I tried to show how the 'balance of power' shifted in this scene by:

Next time I take on the Director role my target is:

The Sophie Smithson Investigation

What you will learn ★★

To show you understand peer pressure and to create an **INTENTION** of making your audience think about how it works.

What you need to know...

To lead your group in creating a scene that has the intention of making your audience think about how peer pressure can damage lives. This intention should make them ask if they have ever done something bad like this.

You will lead your group in identifying and selecting ideas you want to go into this first scene, how it will fit in with the other scenes you will create, to produce the final destination – a drama that will have depth, a message to its audience and situations to make your audience think.

What you need to do:

- Create a scene at a party. One girl, Sophie Smithson, is wearing old-fashioned clothes that make her look odd and out of place. This person is never seen, however, she is offstage. This allows you to get the audience to focus on the other characters' reactions to this odd person.

- Think of situations that could happen at a party that would draw attention to people being peer-pressured. How does someone get made to feel out of place? Or unwanted? Remember this person is offstage – how can this help you?

Ideas to help you:

Hints and Tips:

1 Why do bullies pick on certain people, not others?

2 How do they make life unbearable for such victims?

3 What's your message about peer pressure?

4 Why don't some people stick up for the victim? Why must you be brave to do this?

How your group will help:

Directors will work with you to focus attention on key moments that will emphasise character reactions.

Acting Coaches will provide motives for the characters in the scene, motives that will get the sort of shocking impact you are looking for.

Example 👓

Laura's group decided their ending should involve their audience. After they laughed at the character offstage, they then turned to face the audience with pointing fingers and laughed hysterically at them. It made them realise what it was like. Point made we thought!

The Sophie Smithson Investigation

Acting Coach Acting Coach Acting Coach Acting Coach Acting Coach 1.1

What you will learn ★★

To show you understand peer pressure and to create an **EFFECT** that defines your characters.

What you need to know...

To lead your group in creating a scene that develops the motives of characters that prove how peer pressure can damage lives. These motives should have the effect of making us dislike these characters, despising their awful actions.

You will lead your group in deepening characterisations, looking at their reactions especially. These roles may be used in other scenes you create, to produce the final destination – a drama that will have depth, a message to its audience and situations to make your audience think.

What you need to do:

● Create a scene at a party. One girl, Sophie Smithson, is wearing old-fashioned clothes that make her look odd and out of place. This person is never seen, however, she is offstage. This allows you to get the audience to focus on the other characters' reactions to this odd person.

● Get your group to use the suggestions in the next column to develop the sort of characters we will despise.

The characters' behaviour must be realistic, reflect actions the audience may have seen – in themselves perhaps?

Ideas to help you:

Hints and Tips:

1 You go along with the jokes about this person just so they don't pick on you!

2 You really despise people who don't take pride in their appearance.

3 You pity people who don't have the right clothes.

4 It is your party. She is going to wreck your reputation!

How your group will help:

Storytellers will work with you to decide the order of events in order to get audience reactions.

Directors will work with you to focus attention on key moments that will emphasise character reactions.

Example 👓

Dan, as Acting Coach, asked the actors in his group what their characters' motives would be for making fun of Sophie Smithson. Why would they despise her? Was it lack of money? Lack of fashion-sense? Lack of friends? With this information, he then helped them come up with a line of speech that showed this.

The Sophie Smithson Investigation

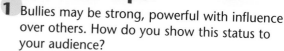

What you will learn ★★

To show you understand peer pressure and to consider how you will establish **IMPACT** in a scene.

What you need to know...

To lead your group in creating a scene that has the impact on your audience to make them think about how peer pressure can damage lives. This impact should make them ask if they have ever done something bad like this.

You will lead your group in choosing where you want to go with this scene, how it will fit in with the other scenes you will later create, to produce the final destination – a drama that will have depth, a message to its audience and situations to make your audience think.

What you need to do:

- Create a scene at a party. One person, Sophie Smithson, is wearing old-fashioned clothes that make her look odd and out of place. This person is never seen, however, she is offstage. This allows you to get the audience to focus on the other characters' reactions to this odd person.

- Get your group to look at how their reactions to this character show us peer pressure. Make these reactions impact on the audience – make them angry or shocked at how people can judge others just by appearance!

Ideas to help you:

Hints and Tips:

1 Bullies may be strong, powerful with influence over others. How do you show this status to your audience?

2 If victims lack these qualities, then show this lack of status!

3 How can you draw the audience's attention to a particular line of dialogue that shows motivation?

How your group will help:

Storytellers will work with you to decide the order of events in order to get audience reactions.

Acting Coaches will provide motives for the characters in the scene, motives that will get the sort of shocking impact you are looking for.

Example 👓

Alice's decision as Director was to draw attention to two characters pretending to read a book out loud but really commenting on the character.

Director Director Director D 1.1

The Sophie Smithson Investigation

Storyteller Storyteller Storyteller **S** 1.2

What you will learn ★★

To produce the right setting (context) for **PEER PRESSURE** as a theme.

What you need to know...

To lead your group in creating a scene that has the intention of making your audience think about how peer pressure can damage lives. The intention this time is to show this theme through the action of your characters.

You will lead your group in identifying and selecting ideas that show how certain types of characters will react differently to applying peer pressure or having it applied to them. In this way your audience may recognise a situation they have experienced themselves and relate to it.

What you need to do:

- Create a scene in a classroom. Sophie Smithson has left the room with the teacher, to show the Head teacher her fantastic History project. The characters left behind have different feelings towards her. What happens while she and teacher are out of the room?

- Think of situations that arise out of spite, resentment and jealousy. Others will just want to make an outsider suffer. But they all intend to be spiteful and vindictive. It is just a question of how spiteful!

Ideas to help you:

Hints and Tips:

1 You will need to read the Sophie Smithson diary which will show how she has already been victimised.

2 Some suggestions of objects found: a birthday card, merit certificate, her mobile phone and a fashion catalogue. Now work with the Acting Coach to link these objects with the characters. What would they do with these objects?

How your group will help:

Directors will work with you to focus attention on communicating reactions of the characters to the 'tricks'.

Acting Coaches will provide motives for the characters in the scene, motives that will explain the degree of their involvement in these spiteful games.

Peer Assessment:

How have other Storytellers delivered their group's intention?

Consider:

a) How clear is their 'message' about peer pressure – so you can explain it in one sentence?

b) Does the situation they created allow each character a chance to show how nasty they are, or are the characters all the same?

c) Has the Storyteller organised this scene so you feel sorry for Sophie?

Rate each section on a scale from 1 to 5 and be ready to give your reasons for rating it this way.

The Sophie Smithson Investigation

What you will learn ★★

To show you understand peer pressure and help **DEFINE CHARACTERS** with motives who use peer pressure differently.

What you need to know...

To lead your group in creating a scene that develops the motives of characters that prove how peer pressure can damage lives. These motives should have the effect of making us dislike them because of their spiteful behaviour towards Sophie.

You will lead your group in creating characterisations that come from their motives. These roles will be used in other scenes you create, to arrive at your final destination – a drama that will make the audience feel sorry for our central character: Sophie Smithson.

What you need to do:

- Create a scene in a classroom. Sophie Smithson has left the room with the teacher, to show the Head teacher her fantastic History project. The characters left behind have different feelings towards her. What happens while she and teacher are out of the room?

- Get your group to think of motives that make them feel different degrees of pleasure at playing nasty, vindictive games on Sophie.

- The characters' reasons must show why and how much they want to hurt Sophie.

Ideas to help you:

Hints and Tips:

1 You will need to read the Sophie Smithson diary in this book. This will show how she has already been victimised by people.

2 Possible character types to include: 'Bully', 'Easily Led', 'High Achiever/Jealous', 'Ms Sarcastic', 'Fashion Expert', 'Hanger On'.

3 Hot-seat each character.

How your group will help:

Storytellers will organise ideas that reflect this nasty, spiteful behaviour.

Directors will work with you to focus attention on communicating reactions of the characters to the 'tricks'.

Peer Assessment:

How have other Acting Coaches delivered their group's effect?

Consider:

a) How clearly have the characters shown different degrees of spite, when they organised their 'tricks'?

b) How well have they coached their actors to get a strong reaction from the audience? Do you hate the characters or just dislike them?

c) How clearly does each character's motive come across for their behaviour?

Rate each section on a scale from 1 to 5 and be ready to give your reasons for rating it this way.

Acting Coach Acting Coach Acting Coach Acting Coach Acting Coach 1.2

The Sophie Smithson Investigation

Director Director Director D 1.2

What you will learn ★★

To show you understand peer pressure and to consider how you will develop the **IMPACT** in a scene, so we despise the characters.

What you need to know...

To lead your group in creating a scene that has the impact of drawing the audience's attention to different characters' reactions to playing a spiteful trick on someone. This impact should make the audience feel disgusted at the spiteful behaviour of 'the gang'.

You will need to 'mark the moment' to obtain this impact. That means finding specific occasions where you draw attention to this spiteful conduct in a dramatic manner.

What you need to do:

- Create a scene in a classroom. Sophie Smithson has left the room with the teacher, to show the Head teacher her fantastic History project. The characters left behind have different feelings towards her. What happens while she and teacher are out of the room?

- Draw attention to moments when characters pressure others to do something unpleasant to Sophie's things. Make these moments impact on the audience so they are angry and shocked at this spiteful conduct.

Ideas to help you:

Hints and Tips:

1 You will need to read the Sophie Smithson diary to see how she has already been victimised.

2 Think about having one 'marked moment' for each character.

3 How can status help you show the characters creating the pressure?

4 Remember Sophie isn't in the scene.

How your group will help:

Storytellers will organise events that reflect this nasty, spiteful behaviour.

Acting Coaches will provide motives for the characters in the scene, motives that will explain the degree of their involvement in these spiteful games.

Peer Assessment:

How have other Directors delivered their group's impact?

Consider:

a) How well have they 'marked the moment'? Have they created deliberate 'moments' that draw attention to peer pressure and who creates/suffers it?

b) How well have they used status to show who the 'pressurisers' are?

c) How well have they created a scene that makes us feel sorry for the victims?

Rate each section on a scale from 1 to 5 and be ready to give your reasons for rating it this way.

The Sophie Smithson Investigation

What you will learn ★★

To understand that **CONFLICT** occurs when characters have different motives, pitting them against one another.

What you need to know...

To lead your group in creating a scene that 'sets up' one of the gang as they play a prank on Sophie. One of the boys in the gang is made to go out with Sophie, but the gang don't realise the boy really has feelings for her. Some of the gang won't want this torment of Sophie to go this far, however.

What you need to know:

- Create a scene in the playground where the gang is hatching the next prank to torment Sophie. By making one the boys go out with her and then 'dump' her in public, they know this will really hurt her.

- This spiteful 'prank' is truly nasty! Not all the gang want to do something this bad. However, if they openly challenge the main bully they may get tormented as well. Some of the gang may want to prevent this prank from happening but without openly challenging the bully.

- It is a question of who is brave enough.

Example 👓

Vicky wanted to show how the conflict grew by working with her Director, Rachael. As each gang member was 'persuaded' to join in this spiteful prank they joined the bully at one end of the stage. When it came to the boy last of all, he was already standing on his own. Vicky created the line, 'Well, we know who is going to pretend he loves Sophie now!'

! Ideas to help you:

Hints and Tips:

1 Why will the bully want to hurt Sophie as much as this?

2 What needs to be said or done by the bully at the start to explain this situation?

3 The bully's motive won't apply to all the gang. You need to have other gang members on a 'scale' (1 to 10) showing how brave they are to state their unhappiness about this spiteful trick.

4 How will the scene end?

How your group will help:

Directors will work with you to use staging to show the isolation of the chosen boy.

Acting Coaches will show how the past affects the actions of characters in this scene.

Unit 1

The Sophie Smithson Investigation

Character Development
Effect
ARC
Physical

What you will learn ★★

To show how the past creates a **CHARACTER'S MOTIVES** in the present.

What you need to know...

To lead your group in finding 'character arcs' that explain their characters' behaviour. An arc shows how previous experiences make people behave in certain ways – these previous experiences need to be explained (even shown) to the audience. This gives any character greater depth so long as all the information is shown to the audience and not '*internalised*' (kept in the actors head and not shown to the audience).

What you need to do:

- Create a scene in a playground where the gang is hatching the next prank to torment Sophie. By making one the boys go out with her and then 'dump' her in public, they know this will really hurt her.

- Get your group to think of things that have happened in their past that affect what they do in this scene now.

These previous experiences may be linked to other characters (like the Bully) or to similar situations, such as when they were bullied. Memories of situations mean avoiding similar ones.

Ideas to help you:

Hints and Tips:

1 People who do hurtful things sometimes do it out of self defence.

2 Character arcs can be shown by a short monologue to the audience that tells of an important incident in their past.

3 Props can be used to help explain – photographs or a child's toy.

How your group will help:

Storytellers will organise ideas that show the agony of this boy as he realises he has to hurt Sophie.

Directors will work with you to use staging to show the isolation of the chosen boy.

Example 👓

Laura hot-seated all of her group to start with, asking questions that helped them invent details about their past. She focused on finding factors in the past that had made the character what they were today and the actors invented monologues that explained these events.

Unit 1
1 2 **3** 4 5 6
Session

The Sophie Smithson Investigation

Audience Awareness
Impact
STAGING
Tension

What you will learn ★★

To consider ways to use the space on **STAGE** to show the isolation of one of the characters in the gang.

What you need to know...

To lead your group in staging the ideas from your Storyteller that show one of the gang pretending to go out with Sophie. He doesn't want to do this because he secretly likes her. As Director, you need to decide how you will position your actors on stage to show this boy as the outsider with a secret. Every character's position on stage should therefore have significance to the audience.

What you need to do:

- Direct your Storyteller's ideas so that the boy stands out from the others, he's isolated.

- Draw attention to this boy being on his own for much of the time. How will the audience find out about his true feelings for Sophie? You will need to provide some way for the audience to find out what is happening inside his mind.

This boy is one of the gang but as soon as he's suggested for this prank everyone else suddenly deserts him – in case they get dragged in as well!

Example 👓

Rachael used the two ends of the stage to great effect when directing this scene. She had the gang at one end, constantly pointing and laughing at this poor boy.

By turning away like this, Rachael felt it showed the boy's feelings about Sophie.

Ideas to help you:

Hints and Tips:

1 Show the contrast at the start of the scene – when the boy is one of the gang and people hang around him.

When he's chosen, the gang members should then behave like he has a disease, they keep away from him.

2 How do you get across his true feelings, so the gang don't know?

3 How do you end the scene? It needs to end as he leaves to ask her out.

How your group will help:

Storytellers will work with you to decide the order of events in order to get audience reactions.

Acting Coaches will provide motives for the characters in the scene, motives that will get the sort of shocking impact you are looking for.

Unit 1
1 2 3 **4** 5 6
Session

The Sophie Smithson Investigation

What you will learn ★★
To understand how to develop the theme for the Sophie Smithson drama – producing a message about social responsibility.

Stimulus

Your teacher will place you in a situation that will mean you will need to play the same characters you have developed in the last three sessions. You will meet a Detective Inspector from the local police station. The Inspector has arrived because something has happened to Sophie Smithson and you are to be questioned about it…

What to do next:
- Decide what your character's reactions are to the Inspector's news.
- Decide what your drama is about – what we call its theme.

S STORYTELLER

You need to create a scene that shows how the characters react to the news they are given by Detective Inspector Goole.

Some of the characters will feel guilt. Others may worry that they will get in trouble for what they have done. These conflicting reactions will allow you to make the audience think about 'social responsibility'.

C ACTING COACH

You need to help create characters that show their motives for being socially responsible – or not.

Why might someone care for others? Why don't others?

How are you going to show these reasons? You'll need to think of lines of dialogue and actions that show this.

How will their backgrounds affect these characters' reactions?

What reactions will they have to the news from D.I. Goole?

D DIRECTOR

You need to direct the Storyteller's ideas in order for us to really despise those who want to keep their guilt quiet! We should provoke the audience into hating those who don't feel guilty for Sophie's fate.

We need to see them bully others in the same way they have bullied Sophie. Clearly they haven't learned! This could be similar to the behaviour we have seen in the playground in earlier sessions.

The Sophie Smithson Investigation

What you will learn ★★

To understand how to develop the theme for the Sophie Smithson drama – producing a message about social responsibility.

Assessment

S STORYTELLER

Assessment: **INTENTION**

- Social responsibility means the responsibility we have to other people. This scene needs to show how socially responsible each character is.

- Their reactions to the news will show this. Those who don't care will try to prevent others from reporting what's happened.

- How will the scene end? Should the police get to know anything yet?

C ACTING COACH

Assessment: **EFFECT**

- How is guilt shown? Do you need to cry? Do you say things like 'If it wasn't for me…' – what are your face and voice doing?

- Why don't the bullies feel guilt? Or are they hiding it? What do they need to say to show their feelings?

- If they say hurtful things to the 'victims', we will hate them – what might they say?

- How do you identify the bullies and the victims? How are these relationships to be shown?

D DIRECTOR

Assessment: **IMPACT**

- Draw attention to the characters that are not socially responsible. We need to see their selfish and thoughtless qualities.

- We will hate them for the way they corner the weak and humiliate them.

- Bullying can be verbal, physical and emotional.

- Victims may be isolated; you can use staging to make characters stand out on their own. While bullies stay close together.

Our theme is social responsibility – we are responsible for how we treat one another. We have a responsibility to help and care for each other. Bullies don't possess this quality.

Your scene needs to show this. When they find out what has happened to Sophie, each character's reactions will show how socially responsible they are. It might help you to think of your character on a social responsibility scale from 1 to 10 (10 = very socially responsible). How will you show this level? And how will the audience feel about your character because of it?

The Sophie Smithson Investigation

What you will learn ★★

To understand how to develop the theme for the Sophie Smithson drama – producing a message about social responsibility.

Now you have created some scenes about social responsibility, share your work with your 'buddy group'. Watch your buddy group perform their scenes but review the work done by your counterpart: Storytellers review Storytellers, etc.

The idea is to help/advise them while they advise/help you.

S) STORYTELLER

- Do they show people being pressured? ☐
- Do we see scenes showing spiteful actions? ☐
- Does conflict arise from different motives in the gang? ☐

C) ACTING COACH

- Do we get to despise some characters? ☐
- Are the character 'labels' clear to the audience? ☐
- Do we see characters with clear character arcs? ☐

D) DIRECTOR

- Is peer pressure shown in opening scenes? ☐
- Are there moments when characters pressurise others? ☐
- Is staging used to isolate the boy? ☐

(If you have been given 3 ticks you have successfully achieved your assignment!)

Write in this box how you felt your buddy group got across social responsibility.

Now show it to your buddy group. Discuss how near (or far!) you were – and why!

What was the best part of your buddy group's drama? Give reasons for your opinions.

Which scene needed to show social responsibility more clearly? How would you suggest they might change it to make it clearer?

How might they develop this drama further? Where could they go with it next?

The Sophie Smithson Investigation

What you will learn ★★

To understand how to develop the theme for the Sophie Smithson drama – producing a message about social responsibility.

Now you have reviewed your work with the help of your 'buddy group', you need to respond to these comments and work out what you must keep in mind as you now work towards the ending.

You are eventually going to create your own drama that comments on peer pressure and social responsibility. So:

Look at your area of responsibility. Which 'concerns' are likely to be important to you as you create your own drama, given what your buddy said:

S STORYTELLER

CONCERNS

- Provoking the audience to think about peer pressure ☐
- Giving a scene an intention ☐
- Creating conflict the audience believes ☐
- Getting across thoughts and conclusions about social responsibility ☐

C ACTING COACH

CONCERNS

- Using character's motives to achieve an effect, like disliking someone ☐
- Defining characters by starting with labels ☐
- Using character arcs to explain motives ☐
- Using monologues to show arcs ☐

D DIRECTOR

CONCERNS

- 'Marking the moment' to draw attention to key events ☐
- Using 'status' to show power and authority, often with bullies/victims ☐
- Using staging to make space work as a way to communicate your ideas to the audience ☐
- Provoking the audience to give an impact ☐

Thinking about the overall purpose of this drama – to create a drama that makes the audience think about social responsibility – how can you provoke your audience to do this when you come to make your own play?

What scenes have we covered so far that you might use/adapt? What other ideas have you got which you might use?

What do your Storytellers, Acting Coaches and Directors need to do now?

The Sophie Smithson Investigation

Narrative Structure
Intention
CONFLICT
Plot

What you will learn ★★

To realise that **CONFLICT** produces tension and that guilt can be a source of conflict. To identify the factors behind the guilt.

What you need to know...

To lead your group in creating a scene that shows how conflict arises when characters have different levels of guilt. Their guilt will make them behave differently, want different things. These differences bring about the conflict and this in turn brings about tension. But what different things will they want? Some may want to confess their guilt. The principles behind conflict shown here will help you repeat the process elsewhere in the drama. This will help you map the conflict as it develops from the beginning to the end of your story.

What you need to do:

- Create a scene where 'the gang' is outside the police station. Two of them want to go in to declare their guilt for what happened to Sophie. The others must prevent this.

- What factors will make some want to confess? What factors will make others want to prevent any confession? How does each side persuade the other?

- This is not the climax of the story so no confessions can happen, otherwise story over! How can they be prevented? How can this scene show the conflict is not resolved and so sustain tension?

Ideas to help you:

Hints and Tips:

1 This story is about peer pressure. Some characters will have been pressured into hurting Sophie. Now they may regret their actions.

2 This pressure may make them resent those who have pressurised them.

3 How are the confessions prevented? Are threats made? Promises given?

4 The scene may develop as the 'balance of power' swings from one side to the other.

How your group will help:

Directors will work with you to focus attention on staging, using space to show the conflict.

Acting Coaches will provide motives for the characters as they react to the argument that is triggered by guilt.

Example 👓

Vicky as Storyteller had a girl break down and cry from the guilt and had the Bully momentarily feel some guilt.

Her tears made Bully show some sympathy for her, which she then used to show how she blamed her!

The Sophie Smithson Investigation

Character Development
Effect
ARC
Physical

What you will learn ★★

To realise that guilt can be a source of conflict and that conflict, in turn, produces tension. To create **CHARACTERISATIONS** that show this guilt and conflict.

What you need to know...

To lead your group in creating a scene that shows factors which affect a character's actions. These factors will trigger conflict and will arise out of their guilt for what has happened to Sophie.

Factors to consider are a character's background as well as their motivations. Conflict arises out of characters wanting different things and using different ways of getting what they want. The principles behind conflict shown here will help you repeat the process elsewhere in the drama. This will help you map the conflict as it develops from the beginning to the end of your story.

What you need to do:

- Create a scene where 'the gang' is outside the police station. Two of them want to go in to declare their guilt for what happened to Sophie. The others must prevent this.

- Your role is to help your group develop their characters to show how much they are reacting with guilt and why.

- These factors will be affected by their past as well as the present. What has happened before to make them like they are? Help your group decide how much they want to confess their guilt. At least two want to tell the police.

Example 👓

Alice as Acting Coach suggested to Laura that she initially stood up to Rachael's bully character. She had Laura shout at Rachael all the times she had got the better of her in their past.

Ideas to help you:

Hints and Tips:

1 Get each of your group to draw a 'guilt scale' from 1 to 10. Ask them to place their character on the scale and explain why they have made that decision.

2 Lead your group in hot-seating each character to find out their background and motives.

3 Coach your group to invent two lines of dialogue that explain their background and two that explain their motives.

4 Decide who the characters are who will not want anyone to confess. Decide who strongly wants to confess.

How your group will help:

Storytellers will work with you to decide what factors will affect the ebb and flow of the arguments.

Directors will work with you to focus attention on staging, using space to show the conflict.

Coach Acting Coach Coach 1.5

The Sophie Smithson Investigation

Audience Awareness
Impact
STAGING
Tension

Director Director Director D 1.5

What you will learn ★★

To realise that conflict produces tension and that guilt can be a source of conflict. To consider how **STAGING** can show this.

What you need to know...

To lead your group in creating a scene that makes the most of the space you perform in. Your use of space is a way of communicating with your audience, providing them with subtle signals. Space is especially useful when developing tension. The space between characters can say a lot without a word ever being spoken!

The principles of staging shown here will help you look at staging in other scenes in your drama. This will help map the conflict as it develops from the beginning to the end of your story.

What you need to do:

- Create a scene where 'the gang' is outside the police station. Two of them want to go in to declare their guilt for what happened to Sophie. The others must prevent this.

- Your role is to use effective staging to display the conflict between two groups of people who want different things. These differences will lead to conflict, not fights – arguments that may see characters switching sides as the scene develops. Guilt will make the characters behave differently, you must show this emotional 'ebb and flow'.

Ideas to help you:

Hints and Tips:

1 'Ebb and flow' refers to tides – when the sea goes in and out. How do characters' positions on stage change like this?

2 Create a 'set'. Decide a space that represents doors to the police station. Some characters will want to enter, others will prevent them. Hence the 'ebb and flow'.

3 Distance between people shows tension in several ways.

How your group will help:

Storytellers will work with you to decide the arguments that affect the ebb and flow.

Acting Coaches will provide motives for the characters as they react to the argument that is triggered by guilt.

Example 👓

Richard directed, having his 'Bully' stand in the doorway to the police station. He stood the Bully on a step to give her status.

The character trying to get past the Bully was therefore lower and so could be easily intimidated.

The Sophie Smithson Investigation

What you will learn ★★

Understanding how to use the stimulus and theme to help create an Overall Objective for your play.

Stimulus

Having been forced to do spiteful, hurtful things to other people, including their own friends, the members of the gang finally begin to revolt against the gang's leader. These characters have faced police interviews and had to come to terms with their own responsibility for driving Sophie to her death. They have different degrees of guilt but they feel that enough is enough. However, standing up to their leader is another matter...

What to do next:

- Decide how your character will get across the message of social responsibility.
- Decide the reactions you want to provoke from your audience through your character.

These two elements will become your Overall Objective – the 'goal' you need to keep in mind every time you make decisions about your drama.

S STORYTELLER

You need to create a scene where the gang revolt against their leader. BUT, how do you get across the message about the need for social responsibility?

You need to create a scene with '5 Steps' that shows how the 'balance of power' shifts from the leader to others in the gang. Each step clearly shows the power slowly changing from the leader to the rest of the group. The final step will be the climax to the scene.

C ACTING COACH

You need to help your actors identify their motives and work on showing the tension in their characters physically.

All the characters are tense, they don't know what might happen, so will be anxious.

They will need to find ways of hinting their feelings to the audience. They may not dare show their true feelings! They will be watching each other for signs, to time their change of loyalty.

D DIRECTOR

You need to direct your Storyteller's ideas that show the gradual revolt against the gang's leader. They will talk to you about their idea for the shift of the 'balance of power'.

You must 'mark the moment' of each step that the power changes hands.

Each changeover is going to be tense, since the characters are not going to know who is going to win. Many of them will be uncertain who they should stick with.

The Sophie Smithson Investigation

What you will learn ★★

Understanding how to use the stimulus and theme to help create an Overall Objective for your play.

Assessment

S STORYTELLER

Assessment: PLOT

- Who will be the main person to stand up to the bully/leader? The boy who was made to trick Sophie in Session 3? He's got motive!
- In what order will the gang desert? This is vital because social responsibility is shown by those who feel most guilt.
- What will be the ending and how does it achieve your Overall Objective?
- Have a speech that clearly establishes a start to a 'step'.

C ACTING COACH

Assessment: PHYSICAL

- How does each character help show the Overall Objective? When will they say or do this? Each actor will need a specific speech.
- Physical skills need to be subtle so as not to be too obvious. Silences, eye contact, gestures and movements needed here.
- The bully may be erratic, using sudden movements, nervous mannerisms; all this will help build the tension you want to see.

D DIRECTOR

Assessment: TENSION

- Use freeze-frames to set out the 'marked moments', and then bring them to life.
- Mark the moment by using status – those in control can be placed higher.
- How might status change?
- Mark the moment by giving the audience a chance to see all that is happening – allow time for a stare, a gesture, a position change.
- Tension = what will happen next. Remember, keep the audience guessing!

Remember, once you have decided your Overall Objective (the message you want to convey and the audience reaction you want) all the above decisions must be driven by it.

The Sophie Smithson Investigation

What you will learn ★★

Understanding how to use the stimulus and theme to help create an Overall Objective for your play.

Now you have created the final scene to this drama, share your work with your 'buddy group'. Watch them perform this final scene and review what your counterpart has done (Storytellers review Storytellers, etc.).

The idea is to help/advise them while they advise/help you.

S **STORYTELLER**

- Have 5 Steps been used clearly? ☐
- Is the Overall Objective shown? ☐
- Does the climax of the scene keep your attention? ☐

C **ACTING COACH**

- Are characters' motives obvious? ☐
- Do actors hint at their inner feelings? ☐
- Are physical skills used to show subtle forms of tension? ☐

D **DIRECTOR**

- Is status used to show authority and does it change at all? ☐
- Do marked moments show tension? ☐
- Is there time to look for subtle acting such as stares, gestures? ☐

(If you have been given 3 ticks you have successfully achieved your assignment!)

Write in this box what you believed was the Overall Objective for your buddy group.

Now show it to your buddy group. Discuss how near (or far!) you were – and why!

What was the best part of your buddy group's drama? Give reasons for your opinions.

Which part showed their Overall Objective most clearly? Give your reasons.

Which part needed to show the Overall Objective more clearly? Suggest improvements.

How might they develop this drama further? Where could they go with it next?

Unit 1

1 2 3 4 5 **6**
Session

The Sophie Smithson Investigation

What you will learn ★★

To understand how to create a play which affects an audience in a clear way because of the Overall Objective you choose.

Now you have reviewed your work with the help of your 'buddy group', you need to respond to these comments and work out what you must keep in mind as you now create your own original story.

You are going to create your own drama now that provokes audience reactions to the idea of social responsibility. So:

Look at your area of responsibility. Which 'concerns' are likely to be important to you as you create your own drama, given what your buddy said?

S STORYTELLER

CONCERNS

- What intention do you need for each scene in order to achieve your Overall Objective? ☐
- How will the intention arise out of the idea you've had? ☐
- What conflicts occur to drive the story on? ☐
- What causes conflict? ☐
- How does the plot provoke reactions from the audience? ☐

C ACTING COACH

CONCERNS

- What sort of effect should each actor try to create with their character? ☐
- How will motives help create this effect? How will they be shown? ☐
- What character arcs are needed and how will they be shown? ☐
- How can character be shown rather than always being told? ☐
- How do the characters help the Overall Objective? ☐

D DIRECTOR

CONCERNS

- What sort of impact is your Overall Objective going to need? ☐
- How can you provoke the right audience reaction? ☐
- What will your set be like in order to help your staging? ☐
- How will the staging contribute to your Overall Objective? ☐
- How will tension be stepped up in order to build to a climax at the end? ☐

Thinking about the overall purpose of this drama – to provoke audience reactions to the idea of social responsibility – what reactions do you plan to provoke? This will become your Overall Objective.

Which scenes in this unit might help you achieve this Overall Objective? What others are needed?

REGRETS —
the story of Sophie Smithson

Refer to Session 1 information

Characters: Sam, Charlie, Kezza, Copstick, Jiffy and Nutter.

SCENE 1

We open in darkness. There is the sound of a girl crying.
Slowly a spotlight comes up on the centre of the stage and we see
a single, empty chair. CHARLIE enters and smiles shyly at the chair,
acting as though it's a person.

Charlie: Hey Sophie, you OK? It's just that you look a little...

[Noise offstage alerts Charlie to someone's arrival. He changes his
behaviour instantly – he becomes hard, brutal. SAM enters]

© What's Charlie's motive for being this two-faced? How can it be shown?

Charlie: ... ugly!! *[Sam and Charlie laugh. They freeze, lighting change as*
Charlie steps out of the freeze, speaking directly to audience]

Charlie: What? This is a nightmare. I tried not to say anything...
[He rejoins Sam in the freeze position. Lights return to original
setting. Unfreeze]

Sam: Hey, Copstick, get out here now!   *[COPSTICK and NUTTER*
enter]

Copstick: Yeah? What is it Sam? *[Looks at empty chair]* **Oh! The new girl!**

Sam: You're telling me *that* is a girl! Who'd have guessed!

Copstick: Yeah, who'd have guessed, eh? Sam? Who'd have guessed? Huh?

Nutter: Shut up Copstick, stop being a...a... Whatever you are!

[Enter KEZZA and JIFFY, Kezza is showing off a new item of clothing]

Jiffy: *[to chair]* **What is *that* doing here? Don't go near it, Kezza. Cheap clothes are contagious!**

① Reactions show the 'downside' of peer pressure.

Kezza: Isn't that the little toe-rag that oiled her way round old Jonesey to get top marks in English?

Jiffy: Well next time she'd best keep that oil on her hair. I come top in English! Always. Hey, Copstick, here's a test for you. What are you going to say to our little grease-spot here? She needs a welcome to our class.

Copstick: *[Aware all eyes are on him. He has to make this look good].* **Oh yeah, hey Sophie... you're, you're... just... pathetic!**

© How can you show Copstick to be pathetic in trying to look cool? What's his motive?

Nutter: Is that it, Copstick? I'll show you. Sophie Stupid Smithson. Look at her face. Covered in all them scratches and all that muck...

Copstick: What muck? I can't see anything.

Sam: *[to Charlie]* **Watch this! This'll be fun!**

Ⓢ storyteller   **© acting coach**   **Ⓓ director**

Nutter: ... covered in all them scratches and all that muck, I said. Look!

[Nutter hurls himself at the chair, pushing it over and punching the 'face' as he does so, repeatedly. As he does this he calls 'Scratches' and 'Muck' all the time. He becomes frenzied; oblivious he is punching the air. The others laugh, point, and hurl insults]

Charlie: It's a nightmare. Like I said. But not Sophie's. It's mine.

(S) Endings can keep us guessing! Suggest – don't tell! The word 'nightmare' suggests that this is a bad thing we are going to see.

Refer to Session 2 information

SCENE 2

A History classroom. General loud chat, noise, jokes, etc.

Jiffy: *[adopting posh teacher voice]* I simply have to take this outstanding piece of work to show the Head. She'll be so pleased. Now, I *can* trust you children, can't I? *[Own voice now]* Yeah! Right!

Kezza: We have to teach our little orphan Annie a lesson, I think. Who's in?

Sam: Oh yeah! She has *so* been asking for it! What you got in mind?

Nutter: Something violent, nasty and involving scissors, I suggest.

Charlie: Do we have to?

Sam: What's up mate? Got the hots for our little social outcast have you?

Charlie: Me? You have got to be joking! Do I look that desperate?

All: Yeah!

Charlie: Shut up! Come on then, what shall we do? Rob her mobile shall we?

Kezza: Oh, think bigger than that, 'Charles'!

Copstick: What you got in mind, Kezza? This is going to be *so* cool!

Jiffy: Shut up Copstick! *[Pauses. Glances round]* Are you going to tell them?

Kezza: Our little Oxfam model has let it be known that she... No! It's almost too unpleasant to think about. The images. I may need counselling!

Sam: Get on with it, Kezza!

Kezza: OK, OK. Sophie has found the man of her dreams, it seems. She is madly in love with a boy in our class. Imagine, something as grotesque as *that* being with a boy! Images of nature programmes and mating baboons! Ugh!

Jiffy: I get it! We get him to ask her out. They go to Youth Club, hand in hand.

Nutter: So where's the payback? I don't get it!

(S) Simple exposition makes clear the situation at the start. Jiffy's resentment is shown from the start of the scene.

(D) Mark this moment! Draw attention to Charlie. We must make it clear that he likes Sophie here because of what happens at the end of the scene.

(C) Charlie's reactions are crucial here. When does he guess Kezza is talking about him? How will he show this?

 (S) storyteller **(C)** acting coach **(D)** director

The Sophie Smithson Investigation

Jiffy: Never do, do you, eh Nutter?

Kezza: You see, while she is on her sugary sweet, romantic date with lover boy, she gets a surprise. He dumps her. Very loud. Very public.

Jiffy: In front of everyone!

Sam: Oh I like it! I like it *very* much.

Copstick: She'll get really upset. She might even cry!

Sam: So who's the boy? I'll just give him some 'persuasion' to join in!

Jiffy: Oh, I don't think you'll need to do that!

Kezza: No, no need for that. He'll cooperate. Won't he? Charlie!

C How can we be made to hate Kezza here? More clues needed here?

D Mark this moment! How do you draw attention to a point when people pressurise someone into something they don't want to do? Not sure about this?

SCENE 3

A park, there are benches. The kids have been playing football, and Nutter is still bouncing the ball, lost in thought. Copstick is chewing at a fingernail, also preoccupied. The ball bounces away, ignored.

Refer to Sessions 3 & 4 information

Copstick: We can't be blamed, can we Nutter? I mean, we didn't do anything. It wasn't us. My Dad would go berserk if, you know, the police came round. He always says I don't stand up for myself and it'll get me into trouble... I know I don't, you know. But it's not easy... He doesn't understand anyway... But what if the police did... come round?

D How can pace be used to create tension here? Keeping the audience guessing gives them time to think.

Nutter: Shut up Copstick! For once, will you just shut up! I've got to think!

[Silence. Copstick goes to speak several times but looks at Nutter and decides against it. But he is bursting with questions, doubts and fears]

Copstick: Nutter?

Nutter: What now?

Copstick: We shouldn't have done it, Nutter. It was too cruel. It really hurt her. When she ran out crying like that...

C How can we be made to feel sorry for Copstick?

Nutter: Seem to remember you laughing at the time.

Copstick: I know. That was then. But now she's... It's like we... like we...

Nutter: Don't say it! You listening to me? Don't say it!

[NUTTER leaves. Copstick quietly wipes a tear away. Silence. Enter JIFFY]

Copstick: Oh, am I glad to see you Jiffy! Heard anything? Have you?

Jiffy: The police have disappeared at last. Had the ambulance gone before you ran off?

Copstick: Yeah. We did it Jiffy. We caused it all. What's going to happen to us?

 storyteller acting coach director

Jiffy: Now get this straight Copstick. You're as much to blame as anyone. Right?

Copstick: But it was yours and Kezza's idea. You suggested it!

Jiffy: And you joined in. Don't try to wriggle off the hook, you worm!

Copstick: [after a long pause] How's Charlie?

Jiffy: The police took him down the station.

Copstick: Oh God! It'll be me next. Then my Dad'll find out. I'm going to have to tell him. Can't have him get told by the police that I was around when Sophie got killed.

[Exit COPSTICK. Jiffy makes to leave but meets KEZZA]

Kezza: Don't go. I feel awful. Sick.

Jiffy: Don't suppose Sophie feels too good either.

Kezza: What's that supposed to mean?

Jiffy: It's what Copstick just said. It was our idea, wasn't it?

Kezza: Well Copstick had better just watch what he's saying. And you, for that matter. So long as we all stick together, we're OK.

Jiffy: But will we stick together? Copstick can be threatened. I was thinking of Charlie.

Kezza: Charlie's sound. He knows who his friends are.

Jiffy: Does he? The friends that deliberately set him up with the girl he fancied. They make him dump her, publicly, so that she gets upset and blindly rushes into the path of a huge lorry. Some friends!

Kezza: Think of the plastic surgery it saved her!

Jiffy: Oh you are one sick puppy!

Kezza: Oh, get over it, will you? She died. Ah. She didn't look where she was going. She should have got glasses. What are you suggesting we should do? Go crying to church and pray for forgiveness?

Jiffy: You said you felt sick just a minute ago!

Kezza: Because I thought the coppers were going to do something. Now I think about it, what can they do? Wag their finger, say 'Don't be mean!'

Jiffy: You've changed lately. Time was when we had a laugh. Now it's just at other people who don't wear the clothes and things that you approve of. You're like some psychotic make-over queen!

Kezza: Listen to the hypocrite. You seem to have forgotten how keen you were to make Sophie suffer because she got better marks than you. Perhaps you couldn't cope with the competition.

Jiffy: Perhaps so. But at least I'm not some psycho.

C MOTIVE – Is fear of his Dad part of Copstick's reasons for behaving like the underdog?

S Dramatic events cause dramatic reactions. Conflict can arise, even between friends. They are unable to sort out their feelings clearly so they snipe at one another.

C What are Kezza's motives for acting like this?

S storyteller   **C** acting coach   **D** director

The Sophie Smithson Investigation

Kezza: Go join Copstick. I'm sure the two of you will be very happy together.

Jiffy: He talked about confessing. Be careful we don't all do the same Kezza!

[Exit JIFFY. Kezza sits thoughtfully, fetches the football and bounces it similarly to how Nutter did. Enter SAM.]

Sam: Got sent off? *[Indicating the football and Kezza alone on the bench]*

Kezza: Yeah. Apparently Jiffy and Copstick are giving me the red card.

Sam: What do you mean?

Kezza: Apparently, it's all my fault Sophie died tonight. You thought it was yours too? Nope. All mine. Sophie laid out on the mortuary slab – all my doing. I think if you check your History book, you'll see I caused World War Two as well!

Sam: Just ignore them! They're frightened. Being interviewed by the coppers like that – they lose their nerve. You just have to tough it out.

Kezza: Right. 'Cos you're doing that SO well!

Sam: It's Charlie I'm thinking of. He's my best mate! Did you see his face when that Inspector made him get in the cop car?

Kezza: Will he say anything?

Sam: Charlie? No! He's sound as a pound is Charlie. And we're his mates. Believe me, by tomorrow the coppers'll be more concerned about some old granny that's been mugged at the shopping centre again.

Kezza: It'll get talked about at school tomorrow though.

Sam: We'll be the biggest thing since that kid tried to jump off the gym roof that time. Do you remember?

Kezza: Yeah. We were behind that too. We are just two *very* naughty children!

[They both laugh, a little too long and a little too hollow]

I think I'll go find Jiffy. Just make sure she hasn't done anything stupid. You coming?

Sam: No. Charlie said he'd meet me here after the coppers had finished with him. Want to make sure he's OK.

[KEZZA leaves. The moment Kezza leaves CHARLIE enters quickly]

Charlie: Can't believe you said those things to Kezza. Did you really mean them?

Sam: You all right? What did they say? There aren't any charges are there?

Charlie: Did you really mean those things?

Sam: What things, for Christ's sake? Calm down Charlie!

C A chance for the actor to show another side of Kezza here?

S Notice now how Kezza and Sam are in denial. Both are refusing to accept what's happened and instead try to convince each other everything will be fine. This is a common reaction to guilt.

D Think about pace here. Contrast the slow and thoughtful sequence with Kezza and Sam to the speed Charlie brings.

S storyteller **C** acting coach **D** director

Charlie: You, laughing about Sophie. How could you. That is so sick, man!

Sam: You did like her, didn't you? I can't believe it. You could have any girl, why the hell did you choose her, Charlie? Why? I don't understand.

Charlie: That's just the difference with us Sam. You never will understand. She was nice. She could make me laugh and she was always running herself down. Yet she didn't need to. She was clever and funny and sometimes she would smile with those sad eyes... She had been through so much as a kid. She told me once. Mum and Dad were killed in this awful car crash. She had this scar on her neck, which was why she grew her hair long. All her relatives were in Canada but she wanted to stay in this country, so she got put in all these horrible care homes and moved from school to school. And after all that, all she ever got was people calling her names and beating the hell out of her.

> *How will you stage this long speech? Try to 'punctuate' the key words in it so the audience see their importance.*

> *What is Charlie's emotional state here? How can it be shown?*

Sam: I didn't know that...

Charlie: Shut up Sam. Just listen. And after all that, all that grief, when you got to know her, really got to know her, she could make you laugh. I tell you, I couldn't have been that tough. And what do I do? I made her think I liked her. And then I let her down. Because I didn't have the strength she did.

> *This play is about strength and it shows two types – the external and the internal forms of strength. Bullies rely on the external type. What strength do the other characters show?*

[Silence. Charlie is bound up in his thoughts and guilt. Sam is unable to understand, help or know what to say, yet, he tries finally...]

Sam: Look, I'm sorry Charlie. I really am. It's just that...

Charlie: It's just what? Don't lie! It's just that if they aren't as tough as you, then they must be made to suffer. Well Sophie was tough. It was just a different kind of toughness. One you can't see. And you, the stupid cretin that you are, couldn't see that!

Sam: *[now bristling with anger]* I'm going to pretend you didn't say that. You're a mate. You're upset. So I'm going to go before one of us does something we shouldn't.

> *How do you stage these two speeches of Sam and Charlie so tension is shown?*

[A brief stand-off. Both boys glare, not sure what to do if the other reacts the wrong way, both hoping the other backs down first. It is significant that it is SAM who shrugs and walks offstage. Charlie stands, shrugs his shoulders and tries to remove some of the tension he feels. He sinks down, broken. Enter NUTTER]

Nutter: *[gentle, softly spoken, not the normal Nutter we have known]* **You all right Charlie?** *[Silence]* **No, 'course you're not. Stupid of me.** *[Silence]* **I don't suppose saying anything like...** *[Charlie looks up at him, daring him to say 'Sorry']*... **No, it wouldn't help would it?** *[Silence]*

> *Allow Nutter time to take this speech slowly, to get our sympathy. Why has he changed?*

[Charlie stands up]

Charlie: We're past apologies Nutter. Now's the time to do something about it. To stop this bullying, once and for all. It's about time someone else showed some strength.

 storyteller acting coach director

Nutter: What are you going to do Charlie? *[Half afraid of the answer]*

Charlie: I'm going to the police station Nutter. I've got a statement to make.

Nutter: What sort of statement? I don't understand... Oh no! You can't Charlie! You can't. Think what Sam'll do! *[But Charlie is going!]* **Charlie, don't do it!** *[Exit NUTTER, hurriedly].*

S Duologues like this allow us to see the 'true' characters, not the act they put on in front of the gang.

SCENE 4

The gang [minus Charlie] outside the doors to the Police Station.

Refer to Session 4 & 6 information

Sam: We're agreed then. Charlie isn't going in.

Kezza: When he sees us here he'll see sense. He has to.

Nutter: I don't know, he looked pretty certain to me. What did you say to get him so upset and angry Sam?

Sam: Me? I didn't do anything!

Kezza: I can't believe he liked that little tramp.

Jiffy: Because you couldn't stand her, doesn't mean we all had to copy you.

Nutter: *[To Copstick, who has clearly been crying and has been quiet]* **You OK?**

Copstick: Yeah. No. I've never seen my Dad that angry, Nutter! Do you think I'll be able to go back home later? When he's calmed down?

Nutter: Come round our place after, if you like.

Jiffy: *[who's been keeping lookout]* **Here he comes!**

[Enter CHARLIE. He sums up the situation, shakes his head, stands in front of the other gang members who, by now, have arranged themselves behind Sam and Kezza].

C How can Copstick get our sympathy? How does this speech provide him with a motive for later when he switches sides?

D Reactions and staging are essential here. We must see everyone react – and react differently

Sam: You're not going in Charlie.

Charlie: Too much like the shoot out at the OK Corral, isn't it?

Kezza: We don't want trouble Charlie.

Charlie: Bit too late for that Kezza. A girl is dead because of what we did.

Kezza: That wasn't up to us! Where do you get off with all this guilt? She ran out into the road. We didn't make her do it. You weren't driving the lorry! It was an accident.

Charlie: But accidents can be avoided. Accidents are caused by something. If we hadn't played that awful trick on her, she wouldn't have run into the road.

Sam: And how does telling the coppers help?

Charlie: It makes it right. We admit to what we did. We face up to it. We were mean and nasty and spiteful, and why? 'Cos she had no parents and didn't have the money to buy good clothes. SO WHAT!

Jiffy: Calm down Charlie, don't stress!

Charlie: Like you don't stress when people beat you in tests, Jiffy? Huh? But of course Sophie did, didn't she?

Jiffy: You haven't got three successful brothers who you have to follow. I have! I just got jealous. OK?

Charlie: And 'cos you're so obsessed with a bit of sibling rivalry you drive a girl to her death do you?

Nutter: That's a bit harsh Charlie!

Charlie: Is it Nutter? Is it harsh when you beat some kid's brains in because Sam tells you to? Is it 'cos you're jealous too? Jealous they've got brains!

Sam: That's enough Charlie!

Charlie: What are you going to do Sam? Smash your best friend's face because he believes something different from you? Huh? Some friend! You're not stopping me from making this statement. I owe it to Sophie.

[Silence. Long pause. Everyone is weighing up their reactions. Rather surprisingly, it comes from an unusual quarter.]

Copstick: I'll come with you Charlie. *[Copstick steps out and joins Charlie]*

Kezza: *[laughs]* Now Robin joins Batman! Don't be so stupid. Do you want to be without any friends? Can you guess what that is like?

Charlie: Yeah. I've spent the last twenty-four hours finding out.

Jiffy: Do you mean that Charlie? We've been mates since juniors!

Charlie: Then what are you doing standing over there? *[Pause. Jiffy looks around, hesitates and then moves to join Copstick and Charlie]*

Sam: This doesn't mean anything. You're still not going in there Charlie!

Charlie: Oh, I don't know. Three of you, three of us.

Sam: Do you realise how pathetic that looks? We can stop you easy!

Charlie: Probably. But when the coppers come out to see what the fuss is about, I won't need to go in. Will I?

[Sam weighs this new situation up. He is uncertain. Kezza tips the balance.]

Kezza: All this because of some freaky kid nobody liked? You lot seem to have forgotten what you are. You're only cool because you get to go around with kids like Sam and me. You three are just loners that get your fifteen minutes of fame because we let you hang around with us.

Nutter: You let me hang around with you? Is that how you really see us?

C See Session 6. Characters' reactions from now on must convey their motives for changing sides. We should see from faces, gestures and movement that Charlie's words are getting through to them.

D What needs to happen in the silence? Tension is vital and so is the surprise when it's Copstick who makes the first move. See Session 6 for ways to 'mark the moment'.

C See Session 4. Conflict is sparked by speeches like this. Also work on Character 'effect' – we must really hate Kezza here, so that we see why Nutter changes sides, and the ending is more effective.

 storyteller acting coach **D** director

The Sophie Smithson Investigation

Kezza: I didn't mean it like that Nutter, you know what I meant.

Nutter: Yeah. Well, perhaps I want to be with friends who don't want to be control freaks. People who know what a friend really is.

[He walks over and joins Charlie and the others]

Charlie: Seems the balance of power has shifted. Now if you'll excuse us, we have an appointment to keep.

Sam: You'll get hassle from the coppers. A lecture about how to be nice. Is that what you want?

Charlie: Yeah. I think we need that lecture. We forgot to be nice for a while. It took you two to show us that.
[They start to move off. Charlie turns] You asked me, Kezza, if I knew what it would be like to be without friends. Well, I think you two are about to find out.

*[CHARLIE, COPSTICK, JIFFY and NUTTER exit.
Sam and Kezza are left staring after them, silent.*

BLACKOUT]

D Staging – how can you leave Sam and Kezza looking foolish at the end?

Tales for a Modern World

Synopsis

Many hundreds of years ago, when women were treated pretty much as servants by men, they had few rights and even less education. Mothers told their daughters stories. These stories, passed down from mother to daughter, always included certain 'truths' that were the important part of the tale. The adventures helped the young girls to remember the story and the wisdom within it. The adventures were also 'in code' so that men, who may be listening, wouldn't recognise the rebellious nature of these tales.

Through the years, often as part of the publishing of such tales by men like Jacob and Wilhelm Grimm, the stories changed and finally became what we now call Fairy Tales. They were never intended to be stories for young children – their violence and horrors will show that to be true! They were, in fact, the original 'Old Wives' Tales'.

Therefore this unit tries to use some of the 'Fairy Tales' and modernise them in such a way that they regain their original purpose. It will be for you to understand how these tales can help you create a piece of drama that gives advice for young women in the 21st century – and returns these fables to their original purpose!

Good luck!

SESSION FLOWCHART

S STORYTELLER | **C ACTING COACH** | **D DIRECTOR**

STORYTELLER	ACTING COACH	DIRECTOR
Session 1 Conveying the intention – creating a drama with a message	**Session 1** Making motives define a character and the effect it creates on an audience	**Session 1** 'Marking the moment' to create impact and show meaning
Session 2 Making the audience feel sympathy for a character and the structure to achieve it	**Session 2** Creating possible characters to play and show motives	**Session 2** Making the audience react emotionally to a particular character
Session 3 Understand how conflict arises out of poor communication	**Session 3** Using 'flashbacks' as a character arc device	**Session 3** Understand how staging can comment on communication
Session 4 Interpreting ideas to produce an Overall Objective	**Session 4** Interpreting ideas to produce an Overall Objective	**Session 4** Interpreting ideas to produce an Overall Objective
Session 5 Using 'steps' to structure a tense drama	**Session 5** Defining characters by their physical behaviour	**Session 5** Structuring a drama using flashbacks to convey the passing of time
Session 6 Interpreting a stimulus to achieve an Overall Objective	**Session 6** Interpreting a stimulus to achieve an Overall Objective	**Session 6** Interpreting a stimulus to achieve an Overall Objective

'**Marking the moment**' may be understood by some Drama teachers, but let us just clarify it for those who don't know what we mean by this phrase. It is a question of 'slowing down time' in order to focus attention upon very specific, precise detail.

It reminds students that anyone watching their work needs to pick up signals, rather than move through a drama with the speed of an express train. This is a concept many, less experienced drama students forget – they know what is happening but they don't consider an audience enough. It is often worth modelling the directing of such a moment, getting actors to consider slowing down performances to concentrate on a gesture, a change of position on stage and a look – while only three or four words are said. We have used 'marking the moment' quite a lot in the early parts of this unit to concentrate ways of teaching, quite explicitly, matters that are aimed at the audience.

The Script: 'Goldie and the Behrs' has been written with the intention of showing how a 'fairy tale' can be updated and made relevant. It has several points that we hope will make it a useful resource for teachers and students:

1. It shows how its Overall Objective is established and delivered, with some of the annotations spelling it out.

2. It provides simple instructions to show how staging can help convey the passage of time (not an issue taught explicitly within this unit).

3. It may help as a stimulus to students who cannot grasp the concept of interpretation easily – therefore it could become Session 1 quite easily.

It can also, as we have explained in the Introduction to this book, be used as a Scripted Performance in AQA's GCSE course. We have tried to build in moments that will provide a chance for all actors to stretch their acting muscles. It can, of course, be added to or changed, in whatever way is needed.

Peer and Self Assessment Opportunities (Sessions 2, 4 and 6)

Later in this unit can be found 'assessment frames' which encourage reflection by students on what they have learned. These frames are linked to the roles students have taken as Storytellers, Acting Coaches and Directors. They are also linked to the learning that has taken place in specific sessions.

In two of the Sessions (2 and 6) there are explicit assessments shown. Activities are provided that encourage buddy assessment – where students review the work of someone with the same responsibility as themselves. The Peer Review Frames:

- Establish the criteria by which the work will be reviewed (based on what has been explicitly taught in that session).

- Allow opportunities for the buddy to explain their thinking behind the point score they have awarded.

- Provide the buddy with a chance to suggest targets their partner may want to follow up in subsequent sessions, again using the learning that has been explicitly taught in that session.

Buddy assessments are very useful as a way of getting students to review their learning in a supportive environment. Since the learning is so explicit, the review of it is achieved simply because they have both been given the same brief and the same learning experiences. We find that, when well established, it is a practice our students carry out themselves as part of the polishing process.

There are also opportunities for Self Assessment, in the Unit Review Frames for the three responsibilities. These Frames may well be used at the end of the unit for students to identify specifically what they, *personally*, have achieved in the sessions. They identify the explicit learning that was relevant for their role in those sessions. For some students, who find it difficult to remember over a lengthy period of time, we find it best to get them to review their work at the end of each session. They can then get a detailed overview of what they have achieved over the period of time the unit has run.

These Review Frames also have opportunities for students to use the learning they have covered, to set themselves targets for next time they take on that leadership role.

By making the learning in their drama so explicit, it makes it easier for students to reflect on what they have achieved. This provides high levels of motivation and satisfaction when well established.

An Outline of this Unit

A Little Bit of History

Don't be put off by any idea that a unit about Fairy Tales is going to be childish and patronising, or well below the sort of work you should be doing in Key Stage 4.

As the synopsis on the first page of this unit tells you, the original stories (Old Wives' Tales, as they were once known) were actually aimed at young women your age. This is because it would be the age when the young women of five hundred years or so ago would be getting married! It was a clever way for mothers to explain the meaning of life to their daughters. These original tales were rebellious! After all, most of them explained how they might 'educate' their husband and master, who would have been the original male chauvinist pig of the 1500s! No surprise that most of the main characters are young women who learn to live by their wits while dealing with strict, slave-driving masters and husbands!

Look at the tales on pages 65 and 66. See how many young women are just given away to other men who treat them badly. Most of the modern versions of these tales, of course, have princes rescuing the girls. This was all additional invention by people like the Brothers Grimm, who were, of course, men who didn't approve of independent women winning the day. Far too revolutionary!

What will you need to do?

(S) STORYTELLER

You will take the lead in developing the ideas that shape your story so:

- You can convey the intention of showing how some young men may behave in a predatory way, like animals, or how young women can be exploited.
- You can explain why conflict arises out of poor communication and leads to assumptions and prejudice.
- You can work with your Director to 'step' a story, making it progress naturally and contain tension.

(C) ACTING COACH

You will take the lead in defining and developing characters so:

- The boys in your group can create the effect of evil, 'wolf-like' young men who prey on girls.
- Members of your group can create the effect of horrible, unpleasant characters convincingly, as well as working on this effect physically.
- The development of a character can be shown using flashbacks so that we can see a complete character arc (their past, their present motives and how they end the play).

(D) DIRECTOR

You will take the lead in focusing the audience's attention on:

- Making them feel the emotional impact you want for characters that deserve their sympathy because of their exploitation or their loneliness and vulnerability.
- How staging is used to show a lack of communication between people. We'll work on how distance between people shows why they misunderstand each other.
- How tension can be built into a scene by making 'steps'.

Tales for a Modern World Unit Outline

Production Outline

Session 1: The Tale of Little Red Riding Hood

This session should really make the fur fly! Wolf fur! The girls and boys in your group are bound to argue about what is decided here as we ask the boys to play the modern-day equivalent of the wolf – the boy who thinks he's God's gift and can get any girl he chooses! While one of the girls plays the innocent Red Riding Hood. We will need to hate *him* and worry about *her*!

Session 2: The Tale of Cinderella

How many of you girls feel you are taken for granted at home? Feel that slavery hasn't quite disappeared because it exists in your home? Then this story is for you! It is a tale of exploitation and making the audience feel sympathy for this poor, wretched, over-worked young woman. Let's hope she finds a prince to take her away from all that!

Session 3: The Tale of Beauty and the Beast

Being a carer, someone who looks after every need of someone who can't take care of themselves – it's quite a job. This is a story of someone able to look beyond the horrible and see the *good inside*. It will be for you to decide this drama's true meaning.

Session 4: The Tale of Rapunzel

This is the tale of a young woman who is locked away in a high tower until a prince turns up to rescue her. But first he must climb her very long hair up to her window. Apart from being a good idea for a shampoo advert, this story has several modern parallels. We have focused on the idea that some parents choose to keep their daughters secure and safe at home, so they are not affected (or infected?) by the unpleasant parts of our society. What if others don't agree with this policy? Do they try to rescue the maiden?

Session 5: The Tale of Snow White

Jealousy and beauty go hand in hand in this story – one woman has the beauty, the other is jealous of it! Of course we are talking about life in the make-up room of any television programme you care to mention. That's where we've set our version, anyway.

Session 6: The Tale of Goldilocks and the Three Bears

Why do some people enjoy vandalising, being hooligans? There are lots of ways things can be destroyed. They all have one thing in common – a lack of responsibility on the part of the person doing the destroying. This tale looks at the consequences.

The Script: The Tale of Goldilocks and the Three Bears

The classic tale of the juvenile delinquent who causes havoc in the neat, well-ordered home of Daddy, Mummy and little Baby Bear. The script we have included for you to work on looks at the issue of responsibility in our modern parallel – which we have called 'Goldie and the Behrs'.

Tales for a Modern World
Menu of Fairy Tales

Below are summaries of the original versions of some of the most popular fairy tales. These versions may not be exactly as you know them, but, like all good stories, they have changed over the 500 years since they were first told!

You may find them useful to consider as you now interpret their themes into a modern parallel – in order to reach your destination of creating a drama that comments on the situation of young women in the 21st century.

Red Riding Hood

Setting off to visit her Granny, who lives in a deep, dark forest, Red Riding Hood is told by her mother not to stray from the path.

Needless to say, she does so. She meets the wolf and tells him where she is going. Foolish! The wolf speeds to Granny's house and eats her and quickly dons Granny's nightdress and leaps into bed, just as Red arrives.

Red, who clearly needs her eyes testing, asks all the famous questions about how big Granny's eyes, nose and teeth are. (Not very polite really!)

The wolf eats up Red too.

However a passing woodsman has heard Red's cries for help and turns up and kills the wolf.

With a surgeon's skill he opens the wolf's belly and out pop Granny and Red, feeling just a little 'down in the mouth' we assume!

Cinderella

When a rich man's wife dies, it leaves him with just his daughter Cinderella. He remarries and the wife and her two daughters take over the house, making Cinderella's life a misery as she becomes nothing less than a servant in her own home.

Fairy Godmothers exist purely to get you out of such a mess. Cinderella gets to go to Prince's party bash, having been given the best 'make-over' in town. Instant love as Prince and Cinderella meet, midnight strikes and she's off, leaving behind glass footwear.

Prince turns up next day with the same dainty slipper and, surprise surprise, it fits Cinderella's dainty foot. This is enough for Prince to ask her to marry him.

She agrees, and very soon wedding plans are afoot.

Beauty and the Beast

A wealthy merchant has six sons and six daughters.

A series of disasters leaves him penniless.

He meets the Beast, when stealing a rose from the monster's palace (big hint there?). As a penalty, the merchant must persuade his youngest, kindest daughter to willingly live in the palace with this huge brute.

She agrees and Beast regularly asks her to marry him. She refuses each time but does become fond of this monster. She asks leave to see her father again, promising to come back.

Beast agrees. She returns several weeks later to find Beast almost dead of a broken heart.

She revives him, he proposes marriage again and, of course, she accepts. Flash, bang, crash – a hunk of a prince stands where the Beast was.

Rapunzel

A poor couple have a child who they are unable to support. Desperate to afford to bring her up, their problems are solved when a woman offers to look after their girl, Rapunzel. So they give her away, as you do.

The woman, not the best foster-mother, imprisons the girl in a tower. The girl grows, so does her hair (no hairdressers in the tower obviously).

A passing prince hears the girl singing and they get talking. She tells him of her plight. He tries the locked door to the tower, no good. Next plan?

Climb up the girl's hair, of course! Thank goodness for that shampoo that strengthens hair, eh? He rescues her and they ride off into the sunset, where presumably she went on to film more shampoo adverts!

Tales for a Modern World Narrative Menu

You may want to consider using some of these scenes in your interpretation.

Snow White and the 7 Dwarfs

There is this gorgeous-looking woman who is queen of somewhere. She thinks she's something else and has this mirror that feeds her modesty every day.

Snow White turns up – she's more beautiful, or so the mirror says! Queen not happy. Tells one of her huntsmen to take SW and kill her.

Huntsman can't. Leaves the little girl alone in the forest (so much safer!). The dwarfs find her; look after her because they always wanted a housekeeper.

The nasty mirror tells Queen where SW is.

In disguise, Queen keeps visiting SW and gives her poisoned fashion accessories which SW takes every time. Finally SW falls into a long sleep.

Dwarfs think they've lost their housekeeper. Passing Prince wakes her up with a kiss. All is well.

Goldilocks and the Three Bears

While walking through the forest, a little girl called Goldilocks finds a neat little cottage. Peeking through the window, she sees three bears go out for a walk while their porridge cools.

Goldilocks goes in, regardless of the law, and helps herself to the porridge. (Obviously girls can eat hotter porridge than bears.) She breaks a dining chair in the process and now, stuffed with porridge, decides it's time for a kip.

She falls asleep, having first wrecked all the beds in the house.

The bears return. Probably blaming themselves for not locking the house up, they find the broken chair, vanished porridge and broken beds and the sleeping vandal.

Goldilocks wakes up, seeing three bears standing over her, not surprisingly, hotfoots it out of there!

Sleeping Beauty

A King and Queen have a baby, and at the christening invite all the local fairies (obviously expecting great christening presents!).

Sure enough, presents are given until one big, bad, old fairy turns up real miffed about being left off the invitation list.

She casts a spell – the baby will die on her 16th birthday, pricking her finger on a spinning wheel.

Nice fairy changes the spell so she just falls asleep for 100 years! Sure enough, the 16th party bash and who's at the spinning wheel? Yep, no dancing for her!

Whole court falls asleep until a century goes by, when a passing prince enters the court and does as anyone would do – sees this dead girl and kisses her!

Course, she wakes up and falls instantly in love with this strange guy!

Hansel and Gretel

A poor couple have two children who they cannot keep, so they take them out into the forest and lose them there.

The kids struggle to survive until they come across this amazing house made entirely of delicious food.

They start to eat the house until the witch, who owns the partly devoured dwelling, catches them. She imprisons them but, because she is short-sighted, she can't see who she is force-feeding in readiness to eat for herself.

Gretel talks her way out of the cage to help the old biddy. Old biddy, glad of the help, gets Gretel to stoke up the fire for the oven. Gretel cons old biddy to climb in the oven (as you do!) and slams the oven door. Baked biddy.

Gretel frees Hansel and presumably they binge out on the delicious house.

Tales for a Modern World Narrative Menu

Written Coursework

Option 1

Write a script for your version of 'Goldilocks and the Three Bears'.

- Firstly, you will need to bear in mind all the points made on pages 87–89.
- Secondly, you need to remember that scripts are mainly what characters say. Therefore you must do all your explaining (your message, characters' motives, etc.) in the lines spoken by the actors.
- Try to make your script 'punchy' – keep the words to a minimum, so that they have impact, but make sure explanations of motives, settings, characters, etc. are clearly given for the audience's sake too.
- Use the 'plot' criteria in this book as a checklist when writing a script.

Option 2

Write a 'Response' – as in AQA's GCSE Drama Part 1.

This exercise involves you comparing the piece of work you are creating with another play from a different historical period or setting. The comparisons made should help give you ideas about the way your drama could be performed and the sort of characters in it.

The play we suggest you compare it to is:

'A Taste of Honey' by Shelagh Delaney.

The plot: The play was written and set in 1953. It is the story of a mother and daughter living in Salford, Manchester. Helen, the mother, is a selfish, irresponsible woman whose main priority in life is having a good time with the men she uses to pay for this lifestyle. Jo, her 15-year-old daughter, is consequently neglected, unloved and unwanted. At Christmas, with her mother away from home with one of her men friends, Jo seeks affection and attention from a sailor on shore-leave from the Navy. Needless to say she becomes pregnant. With the sailor gone and her mother still not around, she is looked after by an effeminate young man, Geoffrey. As her delivery date gets near, Geoffrey brings Helen home, to help out. Helen soon makes Geoffrey leave, against his wishes, as she becomes the person Jo will now have to rely upon.

Themes: The comparison with the situations in this unit will be obvious. Here is a story of a young woman in a different historical period who must struggle against hardship. The play was written by a, then unknown, writer just 19 years old. A young woman writing about the experiences of other young women. Common themes could be 'Neglect' as Jo is neglected by her mother and as Cinderella, Rapunzel or Goldilocks are too. 'Predatory behaviour' shown in Red Riding Hood could be compared to the sailor but also to Helen as well. The hardship Jo experiences in her life is like almost all of the female characters in any fairy tale!

Presentation styles: 'A Taste of Honey' broke new ground when it was performed in 1953, with characters speaking directly to the audience or stopping the play to sing a song. Its style allowed the audience to relate directly to its two female lead characters in a way never seen before. It was also honest, blunt, open and frank in its portrayal of teenage sex, at a time when censorship was strictly operated in British Theatre. You may consider the comparisons in the way you want to present your ideas.

Unit Review Frame – Storyteller

Name --- Class ------------- Date ---------------

*In this unit I have been responsible for leading my group in developing the **Narrative Structure** of our drama. This has meant working on producing ideas that help tell the story in such a way that showed our thoughts about advice for young women in the 21st century. I have learned:*

INTENTION: *(when you set out to create a story/drama with a message)*

1. (Session 1) I helped my group show how the boy in the story behaves like a wolf:

2. (Session 2) I helped my group show how people can be exploited:

CONFLICT: *(finding ways to show differences in opinion, motives, attitudes and the way it affects the narrative (story) of the drama)*

3. (Session 3) I have shown how distance onstage shows conflict:

PLOT: *(how you structure or shape a drama to make a point)*

4. (Session 5) I have 'stepped' a scene, building in tension:

The thing I am most pleased I have achieved is:

Next time I take on the Storyteller role I am going to try to improve:

Unit Review Frame Storyteller

Unit Review Frame – Acting Coach

C Name _____ Class _____ Date _____

*In this unit I have been responsible for leading my group in **Character Development** for our drama. This has meant helping the actors in my group to develop characters that comment on or reflect advice for young women in the 21st century. I have learned:*

EFFECT: *(when you set out to affect how and why the audience sees the character)*

1. (Session 1) I helped my group find motives to create a 'wolf-like' effect for boys:

2. (Session 2) I helped my group develop characters which made them selfish and horrible:

ARC: *(showing the growth of a character, from before the story through to its climax)*

3. (Session 3) Where I showed a character by using 'flashbacks':

PHYSICAL: *(the skills you use to communicate your character to the audience)*

4. (Session 5) You need motives to explain why your character does things. I learned:

The thing I am most pleased I have achieved is:

Next time I take on the Acting Coach role I am going to try to improve:

Unit Review Frame – Director

Name _____ Class _____ Date _____

*In this unit I have been responsible for leading my group in developing **Audience Awareness** for our drama. This has meant working on getting our message about advice for young women in the 21st century across to the audience clearly. I have learned:*

IMPACT: *(where you set out how your want your audience to react)*

1. (Session 1) Marking the moment to show someone's vulnerability:

2. (Session 2) Marking the moment to create sympathy for a character:

STAGING: *(using the space onstage to communicate with the audience)*

3. (Session 3) I used staging to show distance and how it reflects poor communication:

TENSION: *(creating situations that make your audience wonder what will happen next)*

4. (Session 5) I have 'stepped' the tension in a scene:

The thing I am most pleased I have achieved is:

Next time I take on the Director role I am going to try to improve:

Unit Review Frame Director

Tales for a Modern World

What you will learn ★★

To understand that a 'fairy tale' has a deeper meaning and to convey the **INTENTION** that some males can be like predatory animals.

What you need to know...

To lead your group in creating a scene that updates the story of Little Red Riding Hood. You will show the vulnerability of the girl and the wolf-like behaviour of the young male in this modern version. Your intention should be to convey to your audience that some males treat women as prey. Your final destination will be to select ideas that reflect on young women in the 21st century.

What you need to do:

- Create a scene at a party. A lonely girl is seen by a boy who has 'gate-crashed'. She is in danger from him. He attempts to trap her by first getting her alone with him.

- Select ideas that show this young male to be like the wolf in the original story. He lies to her, in order to trap her.

- What sort of comment do you want to make about males in this scene? Commit your decisions into one sentence – what we'll call your Overall Objective. How will the structure of this scene help to convey your views of predatory males?

Ideas to help you:

Hints and Tips:

- What is the boy's motive for his predatory behaviour?

- Beginnings – how do you establish the girl is not so interested in the boy and that he is the problem?

- Endings – what happens to the girl?

- All the characters need to help achieve your Overall Objective – the message!

How your group will help:

Directors will 'mark the moment' that shows the girl's vulnerability and the male's predatory behaviour.

Acting Coaches will provide motives that make us despise the male and feel sympathy for the girl.

Example 👓

Carly invented the idea of the girl becoming 'prey' by his attempt to drug her drink with a 'date rape' chemical. Much of the climax of the scene showed the girl being tempted to taste her drink. It created tension as we wondered if she was going to drink from the glass or not.

Storyteller Storyteller ⑤ 2.1

Unit 2

1 2 3 4 5 6
Session

Tales for a Modern World

2.1

What you will learn ★★

To understand that a 'fairy tale' has a deeper meaning and to create character motives which define the sort of **EFFECT** we want the 'male' to have on our audience.

What you need to know...

To lead your group in creating a scene that develops the motives of two characters. In this modern-day version of the Little Red Riding Hood story, we need to understand the male's motives for treating the girl like 'prey'.

We must despise this character, hate him for his actions. We must also look at ways to show 'the girl' as typical of all modern women. Your final destination will be to define characters that reflect on young women in the 21st century.

What you need to do:

- Create a scene at a party. A lonely girl is seen by a boy who has 'gate-crashed'. She is in danger from him. He attempts to trap her by first getting her alone with him.
- Decide the sort of 'effect' this male should create. How can we make him 'wolf-like' in his conduct? What motives will reflect this quality?
- Animals like wolves, show no mercy. They are ruthless in achieving what they want. They hunt in packs. Does this comparison work for young men? Will the audience react to this comparison?

Ideas to help you:

Hints and Tips:

- Work with your Storytellers to arrive at an Overall Objective – the statement you want to make to your audience.

  You need to work out how each character is going to contribute to that Overall Objective. Each character's actions count!

- What other characters are needed in this story?
- Do the other girls see the threat?
- Can you work with the boys to develop physical movements that might be 'wolf-like'?

How your group will help:

Storytellers will select ideas that show the predatory nature of some men.

Directors will 'mark the moment' that shows the girl's vulnerability and the man's predatory behaviour.

Example 👓

Kerrie worked with the boys to develop 'a walk' first of all. She got them to walk lightly, making them tread from toe to heel.

Then she got them to look as though they were sniffing the air as they gate-crashed.

Unit 2

1 2 3 4 5 6
Session

Tales for a Modern World

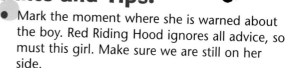

Audience Awareness
IMPACT
Staging
Tension

What you will learn ★★

To understand that a 'fairy tale' has a deeper meaning and to 'mark the moment' where the **IMPACT** of that meaning is shown.

What you need to know...

To lead your group in creating a scene that has the impact, on your audience, of showing the dangers faced by young women. You will need to *'mark the moment'* of key events in this updated version of Little Red Riding Hood.

Moments that will make your audience react to the idea that some males may be predatory (like the wolf in the fairy tale). Your destination will be to provoke an audience reaction when thinking about young women in the 21st century.

What you need to do:

- Create a scene at a party. A lonely girl is seen by a boy who has 'gate-crashed'. She is in danger from him. He attempts to trap her by first getting her alone with him.

- 'Mark the moments' where, step by step, he separates her from her friends and gets her alone. You must get the audience to feel her isolation and her vulnerability.

- Her eventual 'escape' should have the audience cheering! But the lead up to it should be tense with the worry that she may not escape, and suffer as a result.

Example 👓

Keshia used the idea that a predatory animal will corner its prey. Therefore she got Mickel to manoeuvre Lianne into a corner. This was done by frequently invading her 'body space'.

Ideas to help you:

Hints and Tips:

- Mark the moment where she is warned about the boy. Red Riding Hood ignores all advice, so must this girl. Make sure we are still on her side.

- Mark the moment where she is separated from her other friends. How can you use staging to physically show she is alone?

How your group will help:

Storytellers will select ideas that show the predatory nature of this male.

Acting Coaches will provide motives that make us despise the boy and feel sympathy for the girl.

Unit 2

1 [2] 3 4 5 6
Session

Tales for a Modern World

What you will learn ★★

To understand how to structure story events with the **INTENTION** of making the audience feel sympathy for a character.

What you need to know...

To lead your group in creating a scene that updates the story of Cinderella, in order to show how women are sometimes exploited, even in modern times.

The situation you create in this story should provoke sympathy for the central character. Your final destination will be to select ideas that make an audience think about the treatment of young women in the 21st century.

What you need to do:

- Create a scene that updates the story of Cinderella. This is a story of exploitation: a situation in which some women are trapped. What type of comment do you want to make here?

- Select ideas that show your view about this exploitation. Is it fair? Why is it young women who experience it more often than young men?

- Cinderella tolerates it, without resentment. This is why we feel so much sympathy for her. Should she tolerate it? Are things different in the 21st century?

Ideas to help you:

Hints and Tips:

- What reaction do you want from your audience? How do you propose getting their sympathy?

- Once you have answered the question above, you need situations that will provoke that reaction.

- After stirring up these emotions you must provide a satisfying ending.

How your group will help:

Directors will emphasise the ways the girl is exploited by others around her, gaining our sympathy. They will also consider status.

Acting Coaches will provide motives and effect for those characters that exploit our heroine and make her life unbearable, so we end up hating them.

Peer Assessment:

How have other Storytellers delivered the intention?

Consider:

a) How successful have the Storytellers been in creating situations that show the unfairness of exploitation?

b) Can you tell what their message is? Is it clear enough to put into a sentence and can you identify what emotions they wanted to provoke from the audience?

c) Was the ending satisfying? Did it leave you feeling the situation had improved and the exploitation had ended?

Rate each question on a 1–5 scale and be ready to explain your reasons.

Unit 2

1 **2** 3 4 5 6
Session

Tales for a Modern World

Character Development
EFFECT
Arc
Physical

What you will learn ★★

To understand how to define characters by their motives, so that the audience hate them for their selfish, unfair actions.

What you need to know...

To lead your group in creating a scene that develops the motives of the characters in this modern-day Cinderella in order to have a specific effect on the audience.

These characters must willingly exploit people, realising its unfairness, but doing it anyway. Your role is to coach the actors to provoke the effect that make the audience despise them.

What you need to do:

- Create a scene that updates the story of Cinderella. A story about exploitation and virtual slavery. A situation some women find themselves trapped in.

- You need to help the actors become utterly unpleasant, selfish characters with motives that make their exploitation of the central character believable in the 21st century

- Playing 'baddies' is difficult, you may create characters like those in Pantomime unless their motives are real. Avoid the stereotype whatever you do!

Ideas to help you:

Hints and Tips:

- Work with your Storytellers to arrive at an Overall Objective.

  You need to work out how each character is going to contribute to that Overall Objective. Each character's motive counts!

- Is it selfishness that makes people exploit others? Is it ignorance?

- What lines of dialogue and actions are going to convey the motives of these selfish characters, so that they can provoke our hatred of them?

How your group will help:

Storytellers will structure events that portray her loneliness and heartache.

Directors will emphasise the way the girl is exploited by others around her, gaining our sympathy.

Peer Assessment:

How have other Acting Coaches delivered their character effects?

a) Are the 'baddies' merely stereotypes? Do they have genuine, clear motives that explain their unpleasantness?

b) Are there clear lines of dialogue and physical actions that illustrate motivation?

c) How well have the motives and the bad characters helped to get across the group's Overall Objective?

Rate each question on a 1–5 scale and be ready to explain your reasons.

Acting Coach Coach Acting Coach Coach Acting Coach Coach Acting Coach **2.2**

Unit 2

1 2 3 4 5 6
Session

Tales for a Modern World

Audience Awareness
IMPACT
Staging
Tension

Director Director Director D **2.2**

What you will learn ★★

To understand that a clearly defined character can **IMPACT** upon the audience, making them react emotionally.

What you need to know...

To lead your group in creating a scene that has the impact on your audience of making them react emotionally.

You will need to 'mark the moment' of key events in this updated version of Cinderella. Moments that will make your audience react by feeling sympathy for the main character.

Your destination will be to provoke reaction when the audience think about young women in the 21st century.

What you need to do:

- Create a scene that updates the story of Cinderella. A story about *exploitation* and virtual slavery. A situation some women find themselves trapped in.

- Emphasise those moments where the central character should receive the audience's sympathy.

- You need to portray the hardships of her life initially, so what moments can show this? How is the exploitation conveyed? Later we need to feel happiness for her that her hardships have been overcome – how do you show this happiness?

Ideas to help you:

Hints and Tips:

- To gain our sympathy we must never see our main character complain or moan.

- Think of this story in pantomime or how it is shown in cartoons. Her tasks need to show how she is mistreated.

- Status can be used to show the superiority of those who exploit her. This status needs to be seen as a bad thing, it is unfair, unreasonable and even cruel.

How your group will help:

Storytellers will structure events that portray her loneliness and heartache.

Acting Coaches will provide motives and effect for those characters that exploit our heroine and make her life unbearable.

Peer Assessment:

How have other Directors delivered impact?
Consider:

a) How well have they made you feel sorry for the Cinderella character by showing how exploited she is?

b) Have they counterpointed her harsh life with her happy tolerance of it? (As in the cartoons of Cinderella.)

c) How clearly has status been used by the Director to show Cinderella's inferior position in comparison to others in the story? Has this helped gain sympathy?

Rate each question on a 1–5 scale and be ready to explain your reasons.

Unit 2

1 2 **3** 4 5 6
Session

Tales for a Modern World

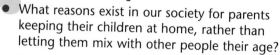

Narrative Structure
Intention
CONFLICT
Plot

What you will learn ★★

To understand that conflict arises frequently from a lack of understanding and that poor communication makes **CONFLICT** worse.

What you need to know...

To lead your group in creating a scene that shows conflict in a story about imprisonment – Rapunzel. You will need to show that walls are not always made from bricks and mortar but from poor communication, prejudice and assumptions.

Here is the cause of conflict. Mapping this route provides you with ideas to help you create a drama reflecting on young women in the 21st century.

What you need to do:

- Create a scene at the girl's home. A boy has seen her at her window and believes her to be a prisoner. He decides he must rescue her, help her escape this prison.

- You need to develop incidents that show how the conflict arises out of both 'sides' (girl's parents, the boy) making assumptions they don't correct because they both think they're right.

- So why is the girl kept at home? Does she want to leave it? Does she see it as a prison? The boy assumes she does, why?

  Does prejudice fit in to this story?

Ideas to help you:

Hints and Tips:

- What reasons exist in our society for parents keeping their children at home, rather than letting them mix with other people their age?

- How do you show the boy comes from a different culture or background, so you can explain his lack of understanding?

How your group will help:

Directors will work on using the space on stage to show the physical distance separating the characters and their understanding.

Acting Coaches will provide flashbacks that convey the girl's past in order for us to understand her toleration of prison.

Example 👓

Lianne's idea was to set her tale in a multi-faith city where the boy doesn't understand the tradition behind the girl's culture.

One part of this scene therefore had the boy accusing the girl's father of cruelty.

The father is furious and they argue.

What you will learn ★★

To explore the idea of flashbacks as a device that provides a **'CHARACTER ARC'** for the audience.

What you need to know...

To lead your group in defining characters that can be used in a modern version of Rapunzel. You will need to show the background of a character, and a good way to do this is to create *flashbacks*.

It allows us to see relevant material from their past that affects their present situation. Mapping this route provides ideas to help you create a drama reflecting on young women in the 21st century.

What you need to do:

- Create a scene at the girl's home. A boy has seen her at her window and believes her to be a prisoner. He decides he must rescue her, help her escape this prison.
- We need to understand the situation the girl is in. Why is she prepared to stay at home? Her background is important and we can see this information through 'flashbacks', providing a *'character arc'*.
- Character arcs show us the past of someone, their motives now. Why and how they change by the play's end.

Ideas to help you:

Hints and Tips:

- What is the girl's motive for staying at home?
- What factors in the girl's past could affect how she behaves today? Tradition? Seeing older sisters do the same thing? A promise made to parents at a younger age?
- How can this event be used as a flashback?
- How will the audience know it is a flashback?

How your group will help:

Storytellers will select ideas that show the conflict that arises from not being able to understand each other properly.

Directors will work on using the space on stage to show the physical distance separating the characters and their understanding.

Example 👓

Carly worked with Keshia to create a flashback with her character as a child, sucking her thumb and watching her big sister get married.

Unit 2
1 2 **3** 4 5 6
Session

Tales for a Modern World

Audience Awareness
Impact
STAGING
Tension

What you will learn ★★

To understand how **STAGING** can be used as a device to represent emotional distance – in terms of relationships, communication or empathy.

What you need to know...

To lead your group in creating a scene that uses staging to show a breakdown of communication and the subsequent lack of understanding in this modern-day version of Rapunzel.

A story of a girl shut away from society, seen as a possession by some, something not to be shared with other people. You will need to decide how staging this will help the audience think about the treatment of young women in the 21st century.

What you need to do:

- Create a scene at the girl's home. A boy has seen her at her window and believes her to be a prisoner. He decides he must rescue her.

- Decide how you will stage this scene so you can show her 'prison' but also allow the audience to see what happens beyond her prison walls.

- Her prison is as much to do with a lack of understanding. How should you stage the characters' positions to show this breakdown of communication? How can distance help you achieve this goal?

Ideas to help you:

Hints and Tips:

- How will the boy and girl communicate?
- When the boy meets those who are keeping the girl inside – how will the distance between them illustrate their lack of understanding of each other's purpose?
- How can staging help show this conflict? Would face-to-face closeness or distance work better here?

How your group will help:

Storytellers will select ideas that show the conflict that arises out of not being able to understand each other properly.

Acting Coaches will provide flashbacks that convey the girl's past in order for us to understand why she tolerates this prison.

Director Director Director ▶ **2.3**

Example 👓

Kerrie used two rostrum blocks to represent the two homes of the boy and girl.

They began by speaking over the phone.

Later, when in conflict with the girl's parents, they and the boy met centre-stage on the floor.

Unit 2

1 2 3 **4** 5 6
Session

Tales for a Modern World

2.4

Stimulus Stimulus Stimulus

What you will learn ★★

To understand how to interpret your ideas in order to produce an Overall Objective that guides all the decisions in the devising process.

Stimulus

Take the story of Beauty and the Beast and update it for the 21st century. A young girl is a housekeeper to a hideously disfigured monster, something so frightening that no one else will do the job. What are the issues that arise out of this story if our destination is to create a drama that reflects on young women in the 21st century?

What to do next:

- Decide what message you want to show your audience.
- Decide the sort of emotional reaction you want to provoke from the audience – do you want to shock? Inform? Challenge their thinking?

These two thought processes will help you arrive at your Overall Objective.

S STORYTELLER

You need to create a story that shows that young women were often treated as 'possessions', servants to their fathers and 'given away' to another man to play the same role. Is this still true today?

'Beauty' is scared of 'Beast' who is hideously disfigured. Yet she remains to look after him out of a sense of loyalty, creating a prison for herself.

In the tale her love breaks the spell that imprisons them both.

C ACTING COACH

You need to use the flashback idea here to illustrate how Beauty has willingly entered this prison.

What are her motives? What has been her background that equips her for such work?

What has she left behind? – Your Directors can use this to 'counterpoint' her present hardships.

How have her previous experiences prepared her for 'rescuing' Beast, so that 'breaking the spell' lets them both out of the prison?

D DIRECTOR

You need to stage your Storytellers' ideas to show 'Beauty' in a form of prison, since she is trapped, unable to leave the helpless 'Beast'.

What happens away from the prison to show what Beauty is missing? How can staging show this and the hardship she must face instead?

We call it 'counterpoint' when the audience sees two different sides of the same idea at the same time. It provokes reaction.

Tales for a Modern World

What you will learn ★★

To understand how to interpret your ideas in order to produce an Overall Objective that guides all the decisions in the devising process.

Assessment

(S) STORYTELLER

Assessment: **INTENTION**

- Being a 'carer' can be like a prison sentence, trapped, looking after someone all the time.
- The qualities needed for this job – are they only found in women?
- In some cultures it is expected of women.
- Is this story always 'happy ever after'?
- Use these answers to form your intention – a message and a reaction.

(C) ACTING COACH

Assessment: **ARC**

- Look at Storytellers' intention and decide how flashbacks will help to achieve it.
- One flashback needs to illustrate Beauty's motives.
- Traditionally Beauty is 'nice' – caring, loving and sympathetic. Show why.
- How will the relationship between Beauty and Beast change and grow in order for them to escape prison?
- Use character arcs to show why they escape.

(D) DIRECTOR

Assessment: **STAGING**

- Look at the Storytellers' intention and decide how your staging emphasises it to your audience.
- Can you stage a prison?
- How will the audience know events outside the prison are outside?
- Your use of space is vital, it can show the distance in the changing relationship between Beauty and Beast. It can show her trapped.
- Use space creatively to stage the intention.

Remember, once you have arrived at your Overall Objective (the message you want to convey and the audience reaction you want) all the decisions above must be affected by it.

2.4 Review Review Review Review Review

What you will learn ★★

To understand how to interpret your ideas in order to produce an Overall Objective that guides all the decisions in the devising process.

Now you have created your story of Beauty and the Beast, share your work with your 'buddy group'. Watch your buddy group perform their version and review the work done by your counterpart: Storytellers review Storytellers, etc.

The idea is to help/advise them while they advise/help you.

S STORYTELLER

- Is the message of 'young women as possessions' clear? ☐
- Is the idea of imprisonment clear to the audience? ☐
- Is 'happy ever after' answered? ☐

C ACTING COACH

- Do flashbacks show character arcs? ☐
- Are motives always shown clearly? ☐
- Does the relationship between Beauty and Beast change and grow in the story? ☐

D DIRECTOR

- Has staging been used to show Beauty trapped in prison? ☐
- Is Beauty's hardship 'counterpointed' with others' happiness? ☐
- Is space used well to show relationships? ☐

(If you have been given 3 ticks you have successfully achieved your assignment!)

Write in this box what you believed was the Overall Objective for your buddy group.

Now show it to your buddy group. Discuss how near (or far!) you were – and why!

What was the best part of your buddy group's drama? Give reasons for your opinions.

Which part showed their Overall Objective most clearly? Give your reasons.

Which part needed to show the Overall Objective more clearly? How would you suggest they might have changed it to make it clearer?

How might they develop this drama further? Where could they go with it next?

Tales for a Modern World

What you will learn ★★

To understand how to interpret your ideas in order to produce an Overall Objective that guides all the decisions in the devising process.

Now you have reviewed your work with the help of your 'buddy group', you need to respond to these comments and work out what you must keep in mind as you now work towards an ending.

You are eventually going to create your own drama that updates a fairy tale to reflect on young women in the 21st century? So...

Look at your area of responsibility. Which 'concerns' are likely to be important to you as you update a fairy tale giving a modern interpretation, given what your buddy said:

S STORYTELLER

CONCERNS

- Creating a scene with a specific intention ☐
- Creating a scene with emotional intention ☐
- Show how conflict is provoked and structure ways to show it ☐
- Creating a theme and reactions out of an intention to achieve an Overall Objective ☐

C ACTING COACH

CONCERNS

- Creating characters with a specific effect that provokes reactions ☐
- Creating 'baddies' that are believable by using motivation ☐
- Use flashbacks for character arcs, motives and backgrounds ☐
- Use flashbacks that help to show the Overall Objective ☐

D DIRECTOR

CONCERNS

- 'Mark the moment' to convey an idea with impact ☐
- 'Mark the moment' to convey a specific emotional impact ☐
- Using staging to convey a lack of communication between characters ☐
- Using staging to achieve the group's Overall Objective ☐

Thinking about the overall purpose of this unit – to update a fairy tale to provide advice for young women in the 21st century – what will that advice be? What do young women need to know nowadays?
This will become your Overall Objective.

What fairy tales might be used to help you achieve this Overall Objective?
(These are just possibilities at this stage)

What do your Storytellers, Acting Coaches and Directors need to do now?

Unit 2

Tales for a Modern World

What you will learn ★★

To understand how to **PLOT** 'steps' into a scene in order to increase tension, and draw attention to the message being delivered.

What you need to know...

To lead your group in creating a scene that updates the story of Snow White, in order to show how women's beauty is exploited.

Your scene will show how the media depend on beautiful women to sell their programmes and how this attitude can promote jealousy and therefore tension. Look at your area of responsibility.

Which 'concerns' from your buddy group are likely to be important to you as you update a fairy tale?

What you need to do:

- Create a scene at an audition for a TV presenter. The male producers clearly want Beauty rather than Brains and the competition is fierce. You need to select ideas for five 'pranks' that are played on the auditioning girls to remove competition – five cunning plans are needed!

- The Snow White character may be innocent and unaware of the jealousy, which will help convey the message about how women are exploited on TV – since SW will be unaware of this exploitation!

Example 👓

Richard decided as Storyteller that one of these tricks would involve switching the make-up of one of the girls.

Richard wanted to make the point that the men in the scene would find it funny, how far the girls were prepared to go. Therefore, even though they could have stopped it, the men just looked on and laughed.

Ideas to help you:

Hints and Tips:

- You need five pranks or acts of jealousy!
- If the jealousy is provoked by beauty then the 'pranks' would try to ruin those good looks.
  Avoid ideas that hurt/damage the actors playing the role of the victim!
- How do the men in this scene behave? How do they exploit the women?
- Make sure you establish your Overall Objective. What emotional reaction are you looking for? What is your message?

How your group will help:

Directors will focus the audience's attention on these 'pranks' in order to increase tension with each 'step' taken.

Acting Coaches will coach the actors on developing the physical behaviour of the characters in this scene.

What you will learn ★★

To learn how to define characters by their **PHYSICAL** behaviour. To consider ways of moving, speaking and gesturing to communicate a role.

What you need to know...

To lead your group in creating a scene that develops the *physicality* of the characters in this modern-day Snow White.

Some of the characters (male and female) may be shallow and only concerned with superficial beauty. Shouldn't this be reflected in the way they walk and talk?

Look at your area of responsibility.

Which 'concerns' from your buddy group are likely to be important to you as you update a fairy tale?

What you need to do:

- Create a scene at an audition for a TV presenter. The male producers clearly want Beauty rather than Brains and the competition is fierce for this job.

- You need to help the actors become shallow, spiteful characters obsessed with their beauty. Not nice people! But work with them to show this physically.

- What gestures and mannerisms could be used to show this? How do they walk?

- How do they show their jealousy in a physical way? Are they all like this or is there one character that is different?

Ideas to help you:

Hints and Tips:

- As models, these characters will need to behave like they are on a catwalk all the time, always 'on show'.

- We need to show the two-facedness of the characters. What must actors do to show they don't mean what they say? How can their voices show this?

How your group will help:

Storytellers will structure events that show the acts of jealousy and revenge.

Directors will focus the audience's attention on these 'pranks' in order to increase tension with each 'step' taken.

Example 👓

Keshia worked with the actors in her group and with mirrors. She got them to work on creating expressions with ultra-wide smiles, wide-open eyes – the sort of things women would need in the false world of the beauty contest.

Director Director Director ▶ 2.5

What you will learn ★★

To understand how to build tension in a scene – by deliberately planning 'steps' that increase tension each time.

What you need to know...

To lead your group in creating a scene that uses tension to maintain the audience's interest and to focus upon the meaning being conveyed.

By modernising the tale of Snow White you will need to show how jealousy becomes a form of tension. Each act of jealousy is like a step on a staircase, taking us to the climax at the top. Look at your area of responsibility.

Which 'concerns' from your buddy group are likely to be important to you as you update a fairy tale?

What you need to do:

- Create a scene at an audition for a TV presenter. The male producers clearly want Beauty rather than Brains and the competition is fierce for this job.

- You need to mark five moments that draw attention to the jealousy and so the tension. Five incidents that need to be thought through carefully with attention to detail.

- These 'moments' will feature an act of jealousy by the girls auditioning, perhaps at another's expense. You'll need to decide where to focus the audience's attention.

Example 👓

Mickel directed a scene where the girls played a trick on one of the other girls. Carly switched Lianne's make-up for fake blood, while the others girls distracted Lianne.

Ideas to help you:

Hints and Tips:

- As Director, you need to draw the audience's attention to the evil plans and keep your audience guessing as to whether the cunning plans will work.

- 'Telegraphing' is when you give your audience hints at what is about to happen. How can you telegraph each of the five cunning plans before they happen?

- Good direction is about being subtle. While a trick is being set up, you must draw the audience to look at it, when characters onstage will have their attention elsewhere.

How your group will help:

Storytellers will structure events that show the acts of jealousy and revenge.

Acting Coaches will coach the actors on developing the physical behaviour of the characters in this scene.

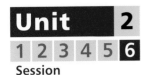

What you will learn ★★

To understand how to interpret a stimulus by creating a plot that reflects your understanding of it and to create an Overall Objective as a result.

Stimulus

Take the story of Goldilocks and the Three Bears and update it for the 21st century. A young girl visits a family home and creates chaos as she destroys everything within it. What are the issues that arise out of this story if our destination is to create a drama that makes an audience think about the treatment of young women in the 21st century?

What to do next:

● Decide what message you want to show your audience.

● Decide the sort of emotional reaction you want to provoke from the audience.

These two thought processes will help you arrive at your Overall Objective.

S STORYTELLER

You need to create a story that comments on why some young people choose to damage the lives of others.

You also need to show the consequences of these actions.

We live in a society where vandalism and hooliganism is common. It is not just the actions of boys either. What are its causes? What sort of punishment should be given?

How are the victims treated?

What is our society like?

C ACTING COACH

You need to coach your actors to convey their emotions and emphasise their motives by using physical skills.

Your characters need to reflect the theme – their motives will do this. But the physical skills will draw attention to the dialogue that explains these motives.

You will need to give good feedback in order to have your actors perform realistically and clearly to the audience.

D DIRECTOR

You need to create tension in this story, tension that comes from the expectation of the trouble caused by the central character.

If your Storytellers want to shock the audience, to achieve their Overall Objective, how will you use tension to build up this shock? You will need to 'mark the moment' when this happens.

How will staging be used to show any lack of communication too?

Tales for a Modern World

2.6

What you will learn ★★

To understand how to interpret a stimulus by creating a plot that reflects your understanding of it and to create an Overall Objective as a result.

Assessment

S STORYTELLER

Assessment: PLOT

- What are the themes here? Responsibility? Obedience? Crime and punishment? How are these themes to be shown?
- Does this theme need a strong reaction from the audience? If so, how is it to be achieved? E.g. do you want to shock? How?
- What will be the purpose of each scene? How will it feed into your Overall Objective? How will the audience know?

C ACTING COACH

Assessment: PHYSICAL

- Look at Storytellers' plot and decide what physical skills will be needed.
- What sort of effect do you want your 'baddie' to have? How will the audience find them convincing?
- What actions can be used, rather than words, to illustrate the characters? Don't rely on words only!
- How will each character help to achieve your Overall Objective?

D DIRECTOR

Assessment: TENSION

- Look at the Storytellers' plot and decide where tension will emphasise the 'marked moments' you have selected.
- How will the tension be 'stepped' in order to build to a climax near the ending?
- What will your 'set' look like in order to help your staging?
- How does tension help you achieve your Overall Objective in this story?

Remember, once you have arrived at your Overall Objective (the message you want to convey and the audience reaction you want) all the decisions above must be affected by it.

Tales for a Modern World

What you will learn ★★

To understand how to interpret a stimulus by creating a plot that reflects your understanding of it and to create an Overall Objective as a result.

Now you have created your story of Goldilocks, share your work with your 'buddy group'. Watch your buddy group perform their version and review the work done by your counterpart: Storytellers review Storytellers, etc.

The idea is to help/advise them while they advise/help you.

S STORYTELLER

- Are consequences of actions shown? ☐
- Does the plot make the theme clear to the audience? ☐
- Does the plot provoke reactions from the audience? ☐

C ACTING COACH

- Is the 'baddie' convincing? ☐
- Are actions speaking louder than words? ☐
- Do the actors' physical performances show a link to the Overall Objective? ☐

D DIRECTOR

- Has staging been used to show tension? ☐
- Have enough moments been marked to convey the shock reaction? ☐
- Is tension 'stepped' so it builds towards a climax? ☐

(If you have been given 3 ticks you have successfully achieved your assignment!)

Write in this box what you believed was the Overall Objective for your buddy group.

Now show it to your buddy group. Discuss how near (or far!) you were – and why!

What was the best part of your buddy group's drama? Give reasons for your opinions.

Which part showed their Overall Objective most clearly? Give your reasons.

Which part needed to show the Overall Objective more clearly? How would you suggest they might have changed it to make it clearer?

How might they develop this drama further? Where could they go with it next?

Tales for a Modern World

What you will learn ★★

To understand how to interpret a stimulus by creating a plot that reflects your understanding of it and to create an Overall Objective as a result.

Now you have reviewed your work with the help of your 'buddy group', you need to respond to these comments and work out what you must keep in mind as you now create your own original story.

You are going to create a drama that updates a fairy tale of your choice, making the audience think about the treatment of young women in the 21st century? So...

Look at your area of responsibility. Which 'concerns' are likely to be important to you as you update a fairy tale giving a modern interpretation, given what your buddy said:

S STORYTELLER

CONCERNS

- What intention do you need for each scene in order to achieve your Overall Objective? ☐
- How will the intention arise out of the stimulus you've had? ☐
- What conflicts occur to drive the story on, and are they appropriate? ☐
- What causes conflict? ☐
- How does the plot provoke reactions from the audience? ☐

C ACTING COACH

CONCERNS

- What sort of effect should each actor try to create with their character? ☐
- How will motives help create this effect? How will they be shown? ☐
- What character arcs are needed and how will they be shown? ☐
- How can character be shown rather than always being told? ☐
- Do characters help the Overall Objective? How? ☐

D DIRECTOR

CONCERNS

- What sort of impact is your Overall Objective going to need? ☐
- How can you provoke the right reaction? ☐
- What will your set be like in order to maximise your staging? ☐
- How will the staging contribute to your Overall Objective? ☐
- How will tension be stepped in order to build to a climax at the end? ☐

Thinking about the overall purpose of this drama – to update a fairy tale to provide advice for young women in the 21st century – what is that advice to be? What do young women need to know nowadays? This will become your Overall Objective.

Which fairy tale best helps you achieve this Overall Objective?

Good luck, as you now start to devise your own drama with these things in mind!

Goldie and the Behrs

Characters: Grimm, Goldie, Jason, Betty, Roger.

SCENE 1

A desk with a chair either side. A tape recorder on the desk. We are in an interview room of some kind. Enter GRIMM. He repositions both chairs, only very slightly, suggesting he likes things 'just so'. Turns on the tape recorder.

Grimm: Thursday the twenty-third, 2.29 pm. Third interview with Goldie Locke. Jacob Grimm interviewing. And let's hope to God that this time it leads us somewhere.

[He stands behind the desk. Waits. Looks at his watch. Waits. He taps his fingers on the desk in irritation. Enter GOLDIE]

Grimm: You're late Miss Locke. Three minutes late, to be precise.

Goldie: I've noticed that about you. You're always very precise. Why is that? Mother a bit of a control freak, was she?

Grimm: This is not about me or my dear dead mother, Miss Locke. Now, please sit down and let's get started. Again. *[They both sit. He is upright and stern. She is relaxed]* Now, this morning we didn't get on too well, did we? Perhaps now you can focus your attention better.

Goldie: My blood sugars were low. No breakfast. I'm no good at concentrating if I have low blood sugars. Are you like that Jacob?

Grimm: It's *Mr* Grimm, if you don't mind.

Goldie: OK. *Mr* Grimm. It's just that it seems such an awfully depressing name, that's all. I much prefer Jacob. I used to know a Jacob in fact. In the home.

Grimm: Which home was that? *[Consulting notes]* Was that the Princess Alice Centre or The Birches?

Goldie: Oh, it wasn't at 'Alice'. No boys allowed there, I'm afraid. No. That was why they moved me from The Birches, I think. Me and Jacob were not good news together. *[She giggles. He frowns at her. She settles]*

Grimm: And it was from the Princess Alice Centre that you became fostered by the Behr family, was it?

Goldie: Not immediately. I'd been to other foster homes before them.

Grimm: None of them successfully, it seems.

Goldie: They don't check up on those people enough. They used to put me with just anyone, I reckon.

Grimm: That's not true, but let us go on. It is fair to say you had some unpleasant experiences in previous foster homes.

Goldie: Suppose you might say.

Grimm: But then came the Behr family. And they were different. Tell me how they were different …

C How can you help the actor playing Grimm to convey the obsession he has with detail?

S Notice here how we compare the two characters to the audience. The reference Goldie makes about Grimm's mother here is picked up at the end of the play, where Grimm tells us the truth about Goldie's mother.

D 'Mark the moment' here. Goldie's speech here is the first time we realise she's psychologically damaged, clearly in trouble, yet she giggles, not concerned about the trouble she is in. How can you draw attention to this?

D How can you stage the transition from this scene to the next without a break? It should appear continuous. Coordinating the set change for the scene is crucial.

 **S** storyteller **D** director **C** acting coach

SCENE 2

Goldie stands up as though to wander around. Various furniture is brought onstage and the Behr home is set up. The interview room remains in its position, with Grimm still sat at the desk, watching and listening. We come to realise this is a flashback.

Goldie: It was friendly and welcoming. Everyone was very nice to me. I remember that when I arrived they even gave me chocolates. Nobody had ever given me chocolates before.

[During this speech the Behr family have entered, Jason Behr holding a large chocolate box proudly. Goldie meets them.]

Jason: I chose the chocolates. I like that kind particularly. *[Points at one in the box]* I hope you do.

Goldie: Thank you. No one's ever been this kind to me before. They look expensive. Thanks, Jason.

[She leans over and kisses him on the cheek]

And, of course, I must make sure you have some.

Betty: We hope you'll be very happy here with us, Goldie. I'll show you to your room, if you like. You can get unpacked and settle in, make yourself at home. How does that sound?

Roger: You don't have to hurry her upstairs straight away, Betty! Let her get to know us first. I'm sure you have lots of questions, Goldie?

Betty: I wasn't trying to hurry her anywhere, Roger! I was only thinking...

Goldie: That's OK, Mrs Behr. I'm not used to this sort of treatment. It's like a hotel.

Roger: But friendlier I hope, hey, Goldie?

Jason: Is she having the bedroom next to me?

Betty: You know she is, Jason. We talked about that. We talked, *very seriously*, if you remember!

Goldie: Is this the first time you've fostered anyone, Mrs Behr?

Betty: Call me Betty, dear. Yes it is. Does it show?

Goldie: Just a bit.

Roger: I'm sure we'll get the hang of it, won't we, Goldie?

Goldie: I'm sure you will. I love it here already. I'm going to feel right at home. I know I will. Right at home.

[There is a slightly awkward pause. Everyone smiles and looks at each other, unsure what to say. Except Goldie, who is eating a chocolate. She returns to GRIMM'S interview room]

Grimm: So it all started fine – at the beginning?

Goldie: Oh yes. Everything was fine then. I loved the chocolates.

(S) What would you say is the Overall Objective in this play? You need to be looking for it as you read.
See Sessions 4 and 6.

(D) 'Mark the moment' of the giving of the chocolates. What is the significance with this event and what happens to Jason at the end? The giving of things – nice at the start, horrible at the end.

(C) How are Roger's and Betty's characters shown here?
Tension exists! Why? Motives need to be clear.

(C) *'Very seriously.'* What does the emphasis on this line tell you? What does it suggest about Jason's motives? How can the emphasis be shown to the audience – vocally?

(D) 'Mark the moment' of the pause. Everything seems happy on the surface but we must show at this moment everything will go wrong. Only Goldie must not appear awkward. Hence the chocolates = relaxation.

(S) storyteller   **(D)** director   **(C)** acting coach

SCENE 3

The sequence that follows should show the passage of time but it should appear rather surreal, with the characters dancing on and off stage carrying various props, showing a normal everyday life in the Behr home. So we see the four of them sit down for a meal, Betty dancing on with plates, the table is cleared, they return and play a card game. Betty, the next morning dancing on with a vacuum cleaner, Jason likewise to do his homework, watch TV. Goldie joins him on the sofa, she messes with his hair and they move closer about to kiss. Re-enter Betty with a duster, Jason and Goldie recover badly, Betty looks suspicious. All exit. The Behrs re-enter, the adults with outdoor coats, wave goodbye. Jason and Goldie, on the sofa again. This time she has a bottle of vodka. She kisses Jason, they swig from the bottle. Roger returns to collect a parcel and catches them. Horror. Freeze-frame.

(D) You will need to decide how to choreograph this sequence to make it look like a dream – it should not look like everyday life. This strange approach will help the audience see we are showing the passage of time.

(S) This surreal dance sequence is a good way to show other events we haven't got time to show via the script but it helps us see how life is developing in the family.

(C) Character 'effect', as we established in Session 1, the events happening now should make us begin to hate the destructive side of Goldie's character. Make us hate her!

SCENE 4

BETTY enters. She paces up and down, clearly waiting. Enter GOLDIE.

Betty: I wanted to have a talk with you, Goldie. While the men are at football. Just us girls.

Goldie: I wouldn't say you were a 'girl', Betty. Not in that little number you're wearing. Nice, but not girly.

Betty: *[hardening]* Yes, well. I wanted to talk to you anyway. About last night. Roger and I were very... disappointed.

Goldie: I wouldn't say Roger was. He seemed far too interested in where Jason had his hand, from what I could see.

Betty: Well really! That is awful... I don't know what you mean!

Goldie: You probably don't either. Led a bit of sheltered life, haven't you, Betty. The way you dress. This house. It's all very neat, isn't it?

Betty: Is it wrong to like some order and tidiness then, young lady?

Goldie: Whatever turns you on, Betty. Now, I think you were saying that you were 'disappointed'...?

Betty: Yes. Yes, I was. I just don't think it's right, what you and Jason were... Well, let's just say, I don't want to see it again. Clear?

Goldie: You want us to do it more privately. I got you.

Betty: Yes. NO!! You know what I mean, young lady.

Goldie: You see, I'm just not familiar with rules in a home like this. God knows my mum didn't care. She had men around all the time. That's why I was taken away from her. That and her drug habit.

Betty: Oh my dear, dear girl. I didn't know, I just didn't know.

[Enter ROGER and JASON. Betty is instantly sunshine and smiles. Goldie remains unaffected as Betty bustles around the two men]

(C) Notice Goldie brings Betty back to the 'telling off' – 'I think you were saying – disappointed?' This shows she isn't concerned about what Betty says. Significant!

(D) 'Mark the moment' here that shows Betty has been 'conned' by Goldie's lies (see final scene). Betty also 'breaks the tension' by being ultra-happy after arguing with Goldie.

(S) storyteller   **(D)** director   **(C)** acting coach

SCENE 5

As in Scene 3, another sequence showing time passing, as characters dance on and off stage. This time Jason and Goldie are doing homework at the table. Goldie seeks help from Roger who stands behind her, explaining something. She giggles and adjusts her T-shirt. Enter Betty as she and Goldie seem to sort out a wardrobe, Goldie throwing away some of Betty's clothes. They are both laughing. Jason enters, in a dark mood, moves to Goldie and strokes her hair, she slaps his hand away. He storms out.

D This should be quite a comic scene, showing Roger's embarrassment. How do you show this? There should be an undercurrent of something nasty from Goldie too – showing how she manipulates other people!

SCENE 6

Enter ROGER and GOLDIE. He starts to set the table for a meal.

Roger: Our Jason thinks a lot of you, you know, Goldie.

Goldie: He's a nice kid. What I imagined my brother would be like.

Roger: Brother? I thought you felt ... differently ... about him?

Goldie: You mean you thought Jason ... and me? *[She laughs loudly]* Jason is OK but, well, he's still a kid, isn't he?

Roger: He's the same age as you!

Goldie: That's physical age. I'm ... I've just seen more, I suppose. You don't spend a few years around my mother without learning the facts of life pretty quickly.

Roger: That's awful, Goldie.

Goldie: Nah, don't sweat it. Doesn't bother me. It's just made me like my men ... that little bit older. More experienced.

Roger: *[embarrassed now]* Oh, well, hmm. Not the sort of thing for a man my age to be listening to.

Goldie: You keep your age very well Roger. I was only thinking that after seeing you come out of the bathroom yesterday. Do you work out?

Roger: *[hurriedly, stumbling over the words]* Work out? Er, no. No. Of course, I play squash a couple of times a month with a chap from work. But no, I don't work out. Do you think I look...

Goldie: I'd say thirty-five if I didn't know your Jason's age.

Roger: Thirty-five? Well, I have always looked after myself...

[Enter BETTY with plates. She quickly assesses the situation]

Betty: You haven't finished setting the table. What have you been doing?

Roger: Erm... nothing. Nothing at all. We were just ... talking.

Goldie: I was just saying to Roger how lucky you are to have him Betty. Such a good husband. Helps around the house so much. You must be the perfect partner, Roger!
[Goldie smiles. Roger squirms]

C Work with the actress playing Goldie to show her pretending to fancy Roger. How does this need to be shown? Jason calls her a tease later remember!

S storyteller **D** director **C** acting coach

SCENE 7

Goldie and Betty enter, dancing with numerous shopping bags, taking out clothes and swaying to a rhythm as they hold them up against themselves. Enter Roger, and Goldie playfully flies a dress over his head, Roger is busy looking at receipts and groaning. They exit. Enter Jason who throws himself down on the sofa.

Grimm: Now if we move on to the evening of the 18th. How did the evening start? *[Enter GOLDIE]* We know that Roger and Betty had argued for some time that evening. Why was that?

Goldie: Roger Behr is mean. He's made her dress in those frumpy old clothes for years. I think he's afraid that if she dressed fashionably other men would be after her. She still had quite a good figure – for her age.

Grimm: So it was about the clothes you had encouraged her to buy.

Goldie: She had no style. I just helped out.

Grimm: And got quite a few items for yourself, too, it shows on the receipt here.

Goldie: She wasn't as mean as him.

Grimm: And after the argument?

Goldie: He went all pathetic on her and said he'd take her out for a meal.

Grimm: Leaving you alone with Jason.

Goldie: Yes. *[smiles]* Poor little Jason.

Grimm: Who was feeling rather left out in the cold after your first 'contact' with him.

Goldie: Like I said, poor little Jason.

Grimm: OK. We move on. It's just after 7.30pm that same evening. Then what happened? Tell me precisely, leave *nothing* out.

Goldie: *[very relaxed, not bothered at all by Grimm's threatening tone]* We sat and watched a DVD. It was boring. Some shoot 'em up rubbish. I got bored.

Grimm: Let me guess, your sugar levels were down.

[Goldie moves over to Jason on the sofa, she starts messing with his hair, as before]

Jason: Give over. You're messing up my hair.

Goldie: You liked it last time I did that.

Jason: That was before you turned into Ice Queen. You're a real tease, do you know that?

Goldie: Don't know what you mean, little Jason.

Jason: Don't call me that!

Goldie: Why not, *little Jason*?

Jason: *[snapping]* Because... that's why!

D Session 3 gives you points about staging. You need to consider these points in how you stage moments like here – where Goldie goes between Grimm's room and the Behr's home.

S Placing this scene here is deliberate. It is setting up to the audience that something is about to happen – it is 'telegraphing' importance. See Director, Session 6.

C '*Little Jason*' becomes a deliberate line Goldie uses to wind Jason up. Physically how can this be emphasised – vocally especially. See Session 6.

Goldie: Woah! I'm trembling, look my knees are shaking. Is little Jason gonna get all manly with me, then?

Jason: I mean it!

Goldie: *[suddenly changing mood]* **God, you're pathetic! Calm down, Jason.**

Jason: So are you!

[A long pause. They both sit, unmoving, staring off]

Goldie: I'm bored. And you seem to be no fun at all, these days. One kiss and you want to turn into flaming Romeo and Juliet!

Jason: I don't. It was… I just thought…

Goldie: It was a good job I found where your dad hides the vodka.

Jason: But, what if he finds out?

Goldie: Grief!! Poor *little Jason's* scared of Daddy finding out! We just fill the bottle up with water. Afterwards… *[smiles]*

Jason: Oh, all right then. *[They start drinking from the bottle]*

Grimm: *[who has been watching throughout]* **So, you had drained the bottle of vodka by 8pm. Is that right?**

Goldie: *[still on the sofa, slightly drunk]* **That's right, old man! It's all gone, little Jason. All gone!**

Jason: *[considerably more drunk than Goldie]* **Is it? I can't get any more out of this bottle. Has it all gone? And don't call me little Jason!**

Goldie: Well, if *little* Jason wants to be big Jason then he knows what he has to do.

Jason: What's that, Goldie? I love you, you know. I really, really do!

Goldie: If you love me, then you have to do something for me.

Jason: What's that Goldie? What?

Goldie: You have to take these. Then we can really get in the mood.

Jason: What are they? Chocolates?

Goldie: Yeah, a special kind of chocolate. They'll help you relax. You need to relax, *little Jason.*

Jason: No I don't! An' I'm not little! Will… will they loosen me up?

Goldie: Oh yes, they'll do that all right. Loosen you right up.

[Jason takes the tablets and laughs. Goldie simply looks at him]

Grimm: And that was when you gave Jason Behr the ecstasy tablets?

Goldie: *[to Grimm]* **Yeah. He didn't *have* to take them. His choice.**

Grimm: Yes. His choice.

Goldie: *[to Jason]* **See? Helping you relax already. So will this.**

C Show here how easily Goldie's moods change. Teasing then instantly irritated and back to teasing again. This shows an unnerving side to her psychology. Emphasise it.

C Work with your actors here to avoid the stereotyped drunken behaviour. It doesn't need to be overdone; a little 'happy' is all that is needed. More so for Jason.

C Work with the actress playing Goldie to show how deliberately she is setting out to make Jason take the tablets. How evil and cunning do you want her to be? How is it shown?

---

 storyteller   **director**    **acting coach**

[*Goldie starts to tickle Jason, who jerks about in an uncontrollable fit of giggles. Suddenly, however, there is a change in his behaviour. His laughter stops and turns into gurgles and his thrashing turns into a spasm that shakes him from head to foot.*
He is rigid now and still spasming]

Grimm: The ecstasy tablets were contaminated.

Goldie: Seems so.

Grimm: What did you do next?

Goldie: Called his parents. They were with us in minutes.

[*We see Roger and Betty arrive – the whole sequence in silence – Betty holding Jason's body which is still spasming. Roger gets on the phone for help. Goldie stands nearby, relaxed, unconcerned. Suddenly Jason's spasming stops, he flops, head to one side. It is clear he is dead. Betty lets out a howl of pain and stares with absolute hatred at Goldie. They freeze in that position*]

S The following stage directions are given because sometimes strong emotions are best shown if there is nothing else to distract the attention of the audience.

SCENE 8

Again, as a dance sequence, not in the family home now but in a graveyard, at a gravestone. Betty lays flowers. She has danced on slowly, lost in her own thoughts. Roger dances towards her, lays a hand on her shoulder. She brushes it away angrily. She cries uncontrollable sobs.

They are both back at the house, putting away Jason's things into a large cardboard box, folding his clothes away. Roger picks up an item of clothing that is obviously Goldie's. He holds it up; clearly asking Betty what should be done with it. Betty stares at it for a moment before charging like a wounded animal at Roger. She takes the top/dress and angrily tears it apart. When she cannot tear it any more she crumples into a heap, sobbing, unable to stop. Roger stands there looking lost.

D Session 6 talks about having 5 steps that show increasing tension. This can be used here – as five actions build the emotional upset felt by Betty, resulting in her tearing at Goldie's clothing as Step 5.

SCENE 9

Back in the interview room, Grimm and Goldie, who have been watching this sequence.

Grimm: You did not tell me where you got the ecstasy.

Goldie: I didn't, did I?

Grimm: I see. Why did you not take any?

Goldie: Don't need anything to help me enjoy myself. I'm just one big party animal.

Grimm: Did you know about the tablets?

Goldie: No. I've never had any go wrong before. Must have been a bad batch.

Grimm: Do you know, Miss Locke, what astonishes me the most?

S storyteller   **D** director   **C** acting coach

Goldie:	No, but I'm sure you're going to tell me, Jacob. I mean Mr Grimm.
Grimm:	You don't seem to care what damage you've caused. Why is that?
Goldie:	Well, it's like this: When you've been in lots of families like I have – seen what they have and what you haven't – you get just that little bit jealous. They are all so, 'Oh look at us! We're so kind hearted, we'll look after you!' They make me sick. They should try going through what I've suffered!
Grimm:	But that is a lie, Miss Locke. You came from a quite well-off family, as I understand it. Though it seems you spin this tale about a drug-crazed mother whom you were taken away from. Quite untrue.
Goldie:	But it's useful to get you out of tight situations. *[Pause]* So what are they going to do with me now, hey, Jacob?
Grimm:	You know as well as I do. A formal warning for drug possession is all we have. They haven't got the evidence to prosecute you.
Goldie:	So I can go, then?
Grimm:	Yes, you can go.
Goldie:	You don't like me, do you, Jacob?
Grimm:	No. No, I don't.
Goldie	*[smirks]* Thought not. I'm not crying and screaming my guilt from the rooftops, am I? You think I should be.
Grimm:	That's right.
Goldie:	You just don't get it. All this has had nothing to do with me. So I let him have some bad drugs. He didn't have to take them. His choice. Not mine. I'm sorry for him. He was a nice kid. But, that's the luck of the draw. It's as simple as that. Luck of the draw.
Grimm:	The Behr family took you in to their home. Gave you everything they could. This is how you repay them – by destroying everything they had.
Goldie:	Then they shouldn't have taken me in. Their choice. Not mine. See what I mean? Luck of the draw. Anyway, see you Jacob.

[Goldie turns and walks out, without looking back. Jacob Grimm watches her leave. Turns off the tape recorder. Tidies his papers, very precisely. Sits still, staring after her. Lights fade. Blackout]

C Grimm's speech is vital to emphasise. It shows the truth of Goldie's background and shows her real character arc (see Session 3 Acting Coach). How do you draw attention to this reference?

S The following speeches help to identify the Overall Objective for this play – to provoke hatred of people who do not accept responsibility for their actions. See how these speeches show this?

C Look at the Storyteller note above. You need to work with 'Goldie' on this speech to make sure she provokes hatred in order to achieve that part of the Overall Objective.

 S storyteller   **D** director   **C** acting coach

Shadowfall

Synopsis

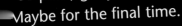

It happened a year ago. You left two friends in *that* house. Every night since then you've had dreams: dreams about those two friends. The police found no trace of them. But you and the other three survivors keep having nightmares about the two of them being trapped in there.

One year later and the dreams become so bad that you wake up nearly screaming every night. You think you see your two missing friends and the guilt becomes too much. You decide it's time to get together and face the house once again.

What has happened to your two missing friends? Why didn't the police find anything about them when they investigated? How can they keep visiting your dreams one year on? Why don't you remember much of what took place in the house?

You call the three surviving friends, only to find they've been suffering the same nightmares. You all realise that the only way to stop the dreams and help the guilt is to return to where it all began one year ago…

You pack, get yourselves ready and enter the house.

Maybe for the final time.

Shadowfall Unit Outline

SESSION FLOWCHART

S STORYTELLER

Session 1
Having an opening image which 'hooks' the audience's interest

Session 2
Using character 'exposition' to explain the plot to the audience

Session 3
Creating a *flashback* to show characters' backgrounds

Session 4
Create situations that make the audience worry for our characters

Session 5
Having a dilemma for the characters to create tension for the audience

Session 6
To understand that *endings* come after a *climax*

C ACTING COACH

Session 1
Using physical performance to create a range of characters

Session 2
Using reactions to show characters' relations with each other

Session 3
Showing the ages of the characters through physical performance

Session 4
'Playing the moment' to create realistic performances

Session 5
Using emotional range and contrast to create a character arc

Session 6
Creating characters of depth so the audience can relate to them

D DIRECTOR

Session 1
Creating a 'hook' to grab the audience's interest from the very start

Session 2
Using *motivated movement* to allow characters to move easily to enhance the theme

Session 3
Using staging to show a different period of time for the audience

Session 4
Creating tension by using silence and slow movement

Session 5
Using characters' emotions to create tension for the audience

Session 6
Using contrast and energy to deliver a memorable ending for the audience

With this unit we are focusing on character motivation and background. By placing the main bulk of the story in the present because of something that has happened in the past, the students can easily see how the one affects the other. This becomes the main learning tool that you can use to guide them to motivation and background with any further work on, or off, this topic.

We regularly ask our students 'why is your character doing that?' and expect a two-level answer: on one level we are expecting them to give an immediate reason for their character's action ('she's coming into the kitchen because she wants to put the kettle on') and on another level we expect something with more background ('she's putting the kettle on because she always has a cup of tea first thing in the morning, since her mother gave her tea when she was a child'). There are obviously Stanislavski connections here, though at GCSE, we do not introduce his work explicitly. It is enough for students to understand that characters need to have immediate and background reasons for being in a scene and that they want something by being there.

Safety warning: 'Shadowfall' is basically a haunted house story. At first glance this can be harmless but it is worth pointing out some religious, moral and personality issues. If there are objections because of religion, where ghosts are seen as a more pagan outlook, perhaps, then the story can easily be altered to one of guilt about two friends getting sent to jail because of something the whole 'gang' did together. Moral issues can be because of recent deaths in students' lives, which clearly need handling with the usual sensitivity any drama teacher brings to a lesson. Personality issues are those where students are easily scared. This means that turning the lights out should be done only when you are sure no one is going to get too scared!

Motivation and background are the main driving forces behind this unit. So that we are clear here, we are assuming motivation to be the reason a character has for doing something. Background, on the other hand, is the character's history before the moment they step into a scene. It is worth pointing out to students that if a play is told in chronological order, then the first scene is background for the remaining scenes, and so on!

Non-naturalistic drama: We have presented some of the sessions in this unit under the banner of 'non-naturalistic' work. How far you feel your students will be comfortable with this concept or performance is, of course, up to you. If you feel we do not push far enough, please feel free to use the whole unit to introduce the idea – with the house itself being played by students, for example, with no dialogue and only movement. As with all our work in this book, we aim to present opportunities for development where you feel comfortable taking them.

Originality: The haunted house concept is so overdone it is arguably impossible to find a new approach to it. This is, in itself, a useful teaching tool. The structure of most haunted house stories is the same (people go into a house that turns out to be haunted and not quite everyone gets out – there's usually a 100-year-old curse on some poor soul who died there) and this allows students to be creative within a tight framework. Fine, you can say to them, stick with the basic structure and that will take care of itself, but you can be creative as to why the house is haunted, or why the people go in there. This is a great way of building confidence in themselves and the story they end up owning. It is also a great opportunity to dust off that old phrase 'it's not the story that's new but the way you tell it'.

The Script: The script here has been written to allow interpretation for the Director, particularly using technical equipment such as lights and sound. The play does not attempt to be gory or exploitative. Our aim is to have a moment's shiver drip down the audience's spine! If students can be encouraged to head down this more subtle route in their subsequent response plays, you will find it far more rewarding than having yet another hack and slash serial killer on the loose. Subtlety for students is one of the hardest things to learn and 'Shadowfall' presents many a trap for over-indulging!

As with all our scripts, please feel free to add, edit, or change anything to suit your groups' needs. The script can be used as a stimulus for Edexcel or as a performance piece for AQA. Numbers and gender of characters are open to interpretation!

Shadowfall Unit Outline

Edexcel work: Early versions of this unit were inspired by the poem '*The Listeners*' by Walter de la Mare. We therefore recommend this poem very highly, as a result! It is a great way into this unit regardless of your exam board, but allows our Edexcel readers to count it as one of their stimulus texts. The overlaps with the unit should be clear from the poem about a man returning to the site of a possibly haunted house…

Peer and Self Assessment Opportunities (Sessions 2, 4 and 6)

As with all our units, 'Shadowfall' presents several opportunities for peer review work. By now it should be clear to the students just how useful this strategy is. Students should now be able to accept criticism and praise in equal measure. We have found that students actively want to be criticised once they get used to the approach. Yes, they love hearing what works well and it's essential that takes place, but students' search for the best they can make it should be apparent early on.

Explicit assessments take place in Sessions 4 and 6, as with our previous units. These assessments are accompanied by the Peer Review sheets you can find in the session details that follow.

This unit relies heavily on the universal idea of a haunted place. This allows students to look into their own understanding of that concept and story and develop their own ideas (in part reflecting the films and computer games they have watched and played). This, in turn, gives them ownership and breeds great enthusiasm.

PS Our advice is that students swap roles (Storyteller, Acting Coach and Director) with each unit, allowing them to develop further skills as they go through the two-year course.

Shadowfall Unit Outline

A Haunted House Story...

We've all heard of them. 'There's a house down that road – never go there after dark.' Haunted houses are a great location which gives you a place for your story to unfold in. This unit looks at one particular story as a starting idea and then asks you to develop different directions it could go in.

Any good story needs to have characters that an audience cares about. To do this we create characters with emotions that a whole audience can relate to. Guilt is one such emotion. We all know what it's like to feel guilty for one thing or another. So, if you give some of your characters that emotion – because they've left some friends behind a year ago – then we, as the audience, can relate to them. OK, we may not know what it's like to leave friends in a haunted house (we hope!) but we do know what it's like to let a friend down and feel bad about it.

From the start you will have an audience with you, wanting the friends to succeed. And that's before you've even shown them the haunted house! This approach works with many different emotions – have the audience connect with your characters in any way and they will follow them through to the end of the play. And into a haunted house, feeling just as scared as you want them to be.

What will you need to do?

STORYTELLER (S)

You will lead your group in the following ways:

- Making the audience connect with your characters' lives and backgrounds. That way the audience will care what happens to them when they enter the house.
- Creating ideas which will make the audience feel scared when the friends enter the house. Hint – lots of blood is not scary! That's a common mistake – scary events are when the audience doesn't know what's about to happen and dreads it happening!
- Grabbing the audience's interest from the start, having them involved in the characters' lives and then worrying what will happen to the characters at the end.

ACTING COACH (C)

You will take the lead in defining and developing characters so:

- They have clear physical reactions, so that the audience can tell what relations they have with other characters on stage.
- Creating a character that is performed with a believability that keeps the audience hooked on the story.
- Using contrast and range in voice and movement to create an interesting personality for the audience to connect to.

DIRECTOR (D)

You will take the lead in focusing the audience's attention on:

- Creating atmosphere and mood that will scare an audience. By using sound, movement and staging, you can make the audience feel scared in their own seats.
- Using movement and staging to make scenes come 'alive' just by the action taking place on the stage.
- Using emotional tension between characters to keep the audience nervous about what is about to happen to the characters.

Shadowfall Unit Outline

Production Outline

Session 1: The Haunted Nightmares

Our story begins at night. The dreams of our main character – Donnie – are seen. He is haunted by the two friends he left behind a year ago. We don't yet know what happened to them, but we do see that they are not happy with him.

But, are they real? Are they ghosts? Or just guilt playing with his mind?

Session 2: The Survivors Meet

Robert's three surviving friends meet up the next day. We find out that they have all been suffering from the same nightmares – when the two missing friends come back and haunt them, telling them that they didn't want to be left in the house. The survivors clearly don't get on, blaming each other for what happened a year ago. In the end, though, they all realise that they have to go back to the house to stop the dreams…

Session 3: What happened a year ago…?

We see a 'flashback' – a jump back to a year ago – where all six friends are about to enter the haunted house for the first time. Here we learn why they were going to do this, how they all got on before the tragedy, and what might have happened. At the end of the scene we see the four surviving friends running away, leaving the two others behind…

Session 4: Breaking In

Back in the present day, we see the four survivors as they enter the house once more. It is silent and no one dares speak out loud. They are carrying torches and all we can see is what they point at. They receive some scares before realising they cannot get out the way they came in. Just then, a door opens and there stand their missing friends. Unsmiling.

Session 5: The Dilemma

The two missing friends are not happy. They realise they were abandoned but not for how long. It seems that time was passing at a different speed for them. Then, much to the horror of the surviving four, the two missing friends tell them that they have to make a choice. Only two of them will be allowed to leave the house. Who is to stay? Who will be set free?

Session 6: The Ending…

With everything they have gone through, what ending could there be for the six friends? Do they all escape the house? Do some decide to stay? What happens to those that stay? All these questions need to be answered in the final scene. And we need to leave the audience with a shiver down their spine as the lights fade at the end…

The Script: Shadowfall

The script we have included for you looks at the pressures on the characters to return to the house. It also looks at the way subtle frights can work as well as big jump moments. The ending has been deliberately chosen as a twist, leaving you wanting more…!

Narrative Menu

You may want to look at some of these ideas to help you choose your own story:

LOCATION

What if the story is not set in a haunted house? What other options might there be? Here are some ideas for where your story could be set:

Abandoned school – maybe something happened to one of your characters' friends in the school before it was closed down?

Circle of stones – what if your story took place near a standing stone circle. That gives you all sorts of possibilities for hauntings, history and horror!

Church – always be careful not to offend anyone's religion, but a church, or graveyard, is an obvious choice for a haunting. The church could have been lost for years and your group of friends only come across it by accident. The story could continue from there!

Railway station – an old railway station is a very atmospheric place to set a story. The number of people that have travelled through a railway station means you have loads of reasons for telling a story.

Shopping centre – normally shopping centres are buzzing with activity. If you take the people away, then the audience expects to see someone jump out at any moment. It has a built-in tension to the very setting. Also, think what kind of shops you can have fun scaring people in!

Deserted town – ghost towns are often seen on films as they give you chance for a lot of spooky moments to frighten the audience with. Think of all the places where people are usually living and breathing. If they're suddenly empty, then the audience feels very much on edge as a result.

TIME

The 'Shadowfall' story is clearly set in the modern day. What happens if you change the time (year or era) of the story? You could easily set the story in the past. The question would then become which year and why? It's always worth remembering that there needs to be a reason why you choose a year for when you set a story. Our version of 'Shadowfall' is set in the modern day so that the audience can more easily connect to the characters and their situations.

If you wanted to be adventurous you could set the story at some point in the future! The message for the audience here could be that no matter how much technology you have, it won't save you from your fears and your guilt.

In both cases – past or future – you do need to make sure that you have a reason for setting it in that time period. Also, make sure you can afford to stage it (costumes are not cheap!).

Shadowfall Narrative Menu

Shadowfall Narrative Menu

You may want to consider using some of these scenes in your interpretation.

THEME

Our version of 'Shadowfall' is about guilt and responsibility. The four surviving characters feel guilt about the way they have run out on their two missing friends. They also feel responsible for what has happened. These are our themes. Here's an example of how you could take the same script and change the theme:

Revenge – the four survivors return to the house so that they can get revenge for their two friends' disappearance. This would mean you could look at what it takes for someone to do something for revenge and how it makes them feel.

Jealousy – the story of the haunted house looks at jealousy. You could do this by having the relationships between the friends even more complicated.

Religion – some of the characters could be religious and the hauntings might be for religious reasons, perhaps? Be careful when you explore this theme that you don't offend anyone's feelings in your group. However, religion is a good way of explaining some of the events that take place in the house.

Loss and grief – how do people cope when friends and relatives disappear? The story could easily be altered to look at the different ways that people cope with grief. The basic story remains the same but the characters speak more about how they feel and how they have dealt with their friends' disappearance.

GENRE AND STYLE

It's clear that 'Shadowfall' is meant to be a scary ghost story. However, even with the same storyline, it doesn't have to be a scary type of story. A play's style is very strongly connected to the Overall Objective. Here are other ways you could think of telling it:

Comedy – 'Shadowfall' can easily be changed into a comedy. It can still have ghosts and a haunted house, but the events that happen can produce funny responses in your characters, rather than scared and scary ones. If you think your group is better suited to telling this kind of story, then look to change our script, or your own version, until it makes the audience laugh. That would then be your Overall Objective – to make the audience laugh at the characters' situation.

Mystery – what if the story didn't involve ghosts? If you decided you wanted to tell a very similar story to the one in our script, you could do away with the idea of ghosts haunting the main characters and just have them plagued by guilt. They then investigate what has happened to their two missing friends and find out their fate.

Naturalistic – most of our version of 'Shadowfall' is written to be performed as naturalistically as possible. In other words, the audience should be able to watch most of 'Shadowfall' and think 'that's so real'. You could look at the script and see if you can make it even more believable, even more realistic for your audience.

Non-naturalistic – you can stage the story so that what happens on stage is not presented in a normal way. You could have characters suddenly stop and turn to the audience to tell them what they are thinking and feeling. You could use everyone in your cast to create the actual walls of the house, the doors and the sound effects. These can be very effective tools for scaring the audience. You could have the actors move through the audience, so that the audience isn't sure when the next scare is going to happen or from where.

Written Coursework

Option 1

Write your own script for the ending after Scene 5.

- Think about where the story is at so far – the four surviving friends have found their missing mates. They have been told that only two are allowed to leave. We finish that scene not knowing what decision has been made.

- Now think, what effect do you want to have on the audience? You can think of this in two ways – what effect do you want to have on them in your version of Scene 6? And, what effect do you want to have on the audience for the overall play? (This last is called Overall Objective – the overall effect you are after.)

- Now consider the different skills you have learnt – creating characters the audience can relate to, subtle events that don't overdo the gore, using range and contrast to capture the audience's interest, to name only three!

Now write your own ending to the play. What do you want to happen? How might it end for all the characters? Are you setting the last scene in the future or straight after Scene 5? You decide!

Option 2

Write a 'Response' – as in AQA's GCSE Drama Part 1.

This assessed work involves you comparing the ideas you have for your drama with another play from another time or culture.

The point of a 'Response' is to help you see why you have made the choices in your play that you have. Most people can understand their own work much better when they think about another piece of work in comparison.

We suggest any of the following plays to compare your own work to:

- 'The Exorcism' by Don Taylor
- 'The Woman in Black' by Susan Hill (adapted by Stephen Mallatratt)
- 'The Signal Man' by Charles Dickens

What to do: See which plays your teacher has available. Read them and choose one play that allows you to compare your own play and character to. When you have written the comparison of story and character, say how you will now perform your character following the comparison.

Option 3

Create your own version of the 'Shadowfall' story!

Use all of the elements that we have covered in the six sessions: hooking an audience into the story, using conflict between characters to keep the audience interested, using 'exposition' to explain the plot, having flashbacks to a time before they went into the house, perhaps. The list is endless! We have provided a range of possible stories in the previous two pages.

Shadowfall Unit Outline

Unit Review Frame – Storyteller

(S) Name _____ Class _____ Date _____

In this unit I have been responsible for leading my group in developing the Narrative Structure of our drama. This has meant helping to create a story which aims to scare the audience! I have learned:

INTENTION: *(when you set out to create a story/drama with a message)*

1. (Session 1) I helped my group create an opening that hooks the audience in by:

2. (Session 4) I created situations which made the audience care for the characters by:

3. (Session 6) I helped choose an ending which fits the Overall Objective of our story by:

CONFLICT: *(finding ways to show differences in opinion, motives, attitudes and the way it affects the narrative (story) of the drama)*

4. (Session 5) I have created situations where characters face a difficult dilemma by:

PLOT: *(how you structure or shape a drama to make a point)*

5. (Session 2) I have used 'exposition' in the following ways:

6. (Session 3) I have created a flashback scene that shows the characters' backgrounds:

The thing that I am most pleased I have achieved is:

Next time I take on the Storyteller role I am going to try to improve:

Unit Review Frame – Acting Coach

Name _____ **Class** _____ **Date** _____

In this unit I have been responsible for leading my group in Character Development in our drama. This meant I have been helping create realistic performances for my group. I have learned:

EFFECT: *(when you set out to affect how and why the audience sees the character)*

1. (Session 4) I helped my group play the reality of the moments for their characters by:

2. (Session 6) I helped my group create characters that the audience felt sympathy for by:

ARC: *(showing the growth of a character, from before the story to its climax)*

3. (Session 2) I helped characters show their personality through reactions by:

4. (Session 5) I helped the group use emotional range and contrast to create depth by:

PHYSICAL: *(the skills you use to communicate your character to the audience)*

5. (Session 1) I helped the group use physical actions to show their characters clearly by:

6. (Session 3) The age of the characters was shown using the following physical skills by:

The thing I am most pleased I have achieved is:

Next time I take on the Acting Coach role I am going to try to improve:

Unit Review Frame Acting Coach

Unit Review Frame – Director

D Name --- Class -------------- Date --------------

In this unit I have been responsible for leading my group in developing Audience Awareness in our drama. This has meant creating atmosphere and mood in order to scare the audience! I have learned:

IMPACT: *(where you decide how you want your audience to react)*

1. (Session 1) I helped the audience become 'hooked' on our story by:

2. (Session 6) I used atmosphere and energy to create the final impact by:

STAGING: *(using the space onstage to communicate with the audience)*

3. (Session 2) I used motivated movement to keep the audience interested in a scene by:

4. (Session 3) I made it clear to the audience what time period they were watching by:

TENSION: *(creating situations that make your audience wonder what will happen next)*

5. (Session 4) I have used silence and slow movement to create tension by:

6. (Session 5) I have used character interaction to create emotional tension by:

The thing I am most pleased I have achieved is:

Next time I take on the Director role I am going to try to improve:

Unit Review Frame Director

Shadowfall

What you will learn ★★

To understand how a '**HOOK**' at the start of a story can make the audience want to watch the rest of the play.

What you need to know...

To create a short scene that shows a character feeling guilty about something they have done in the past. The intention of this scene is to scare the audience just enough to keep them watching!

Concentrate on coming up with a single idea that will make the audience scared of looking at their own photographs later!

What you need to do:

- Create a scene where one person, Donnie, is looking at some photos from a year ago. The photos are of friends who have been lost, presumed dead, in a haunted house they all visited last year. As Donnie looks at the photos they come alive.
- How can you make this scary? What happens when the photos come alive?
- Try and finish the scene where Donnie is left alone, scared.
- The focus of the scene is what happens when the photos come alive. That's where the scares will come from.

Ideas to help you:

Hints and Tips:

- Would they talk to Donnie or not?
- The more an audience can identify with, the more scared they will be.
- Why are the ghosts there? Maybe Donnie doesn't know and has to find out?

Think about what they do when they arrive, why they're there and what they want from Donnie and you should have some great ideas.

How your group will help:

Directors will be finding ways of making an impact by presenting your scene cleverly.

Acting Coaches will be helping the actors create interesting characters.

Example 👓

Carly decides to have the photos come alive and attack Donnie. She doesn't need to decide how this happens (that's the Director's problem!). The two people Donnie has left behind are going to step from the photographs and attack him. At the end of the scene Donnie wakes and he realises it is another nightmare.

Shadowfall

What you will learn ★★

To understand that a strong **PHYSICAL** performance of a character tells the audience as much as words can.

What you need to know...

To lead your group to create a *physical performance* for the actors in this scene.

Two of the three people are ghosts and you will need to think of physical ways of showing the audience this. No one is going to explain this to the audience, so your job is to make it clear from the way they move and talk.

The other person on stage is going to need to be as realistic as possible when the ghosts appear!

What you need to do:

- You will be helping create a scene where a character, Donnie, is looking at photographs of two missing friends. The friends appear in front of him and he is frightened.

- You will need to make the two ghosts be very frightening, just by their appearance and performance. The way they move, speak and interact with Donnie is very important.

- Donnie needs to react as realistically as possible so that the audience knows this isn't something that happens normally!

- The clearer you make the ghosts' performances the more the audience will understand what they are meant to be.

Ideas to help you:

Hints and Tips:

- How would you want the two ghosts to move?
- If they speak, what voices would they have that might scare the audience?
- How would you dress the ghosts – maybe in black and white to show they are from the photos?
- The more scared Donnie can look, the more likely the audience are going to feel sorry for him.

These are not easy things to perform, so be supportive and encouraging to all your actors.

How your group will help:

Storytellers will create a scene where one character is haunted by events from their past.

Directors will be finding ways of making an impact by presenting this scene cleverly.

Example 👓

Richard decides to create the two ghosts so that they contrast with Donnie.

Donnie is going to move fast, in a very natural way, scrambling back on the bed when the ghosts appear. His reactions are very much on his face, so Richard concentrates on getting the actor to perform them well.

The two ghosts are going to move slowly, tilt their heads at the same time and keep their eyes wide open, never blinking.

What you will learn ★★

To understand how a 'HOOK' at the start of a play can grab an audience's interest and give them a sense of atmosphere for the rest of the play.

What you need to know...

You will lead your group to create an opening for your story which will grab the audience's interest – make an *impact* on them. The atmosphere you set for the audience will make them realise what kind of play they can expect from now on.

What you need to do:

- Using the story that your Storyteller has created, think of a way of grabbing the audience's interest from the opening seconds. This is called a 'hook', or 'hooking' the audience in.

- Think about where the cast are on stage, what sounds, lights, props and music you could use.

- You are trying to scare the audience as well as interest them!

- At the end of this short scene the audience should be unnerved but want to watch the rest of the play!

Ideas to help you:

Hints and Tips:

- You could start whispering before the lights come up...

- Or spooky music to set the atmosphere...

- A sudden scream – but what happens straight after is just as important...

Why not try combining some of these for the best effect you can?

How your group will help:

Storytellers will create a scene where one character is haunted by events from their past.

Acting Coaches will create interesting characters for the audience to watch.

Example 👓

Vicky has decided to start the scene in darkness with doors slamming all around the audience. Then, the doors stop at the same time and there is silence except for a breathing sound from someone on stage. The scene continues from here with the audience hooked from the start!

Unit 3

Shadowfall

What you will learn ★★

To understand the term '**EXPOSITION**' and how it can be used to tell an audience what is going on.

What you need to know...

To lead your group in creating a scene which shows the audience what is going on. This is called '*exposition*' – explaining the plot to the audience. In drama this is usually done when characters talk to each other.

The dialogue would show what had happened and what the characters thought. Make sure you don't explain too much, otherwise the audience won't need to watch anymore!

What you need to do:

- Create a scene where Donnie meets up with his three surviving friends. In this scene you will need to make clear to the audience what happened a year ago, why these four people escaped and the other two didn't.
- Think of why a group of six friends might go into a haunted house. Why would they then leave two of their friends behind?
- The trick with exposition is to have enough explained that the audience is interested, but not too much that they don't need to see the rest of the play!

Ideas to help you:

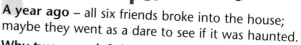

Hints and Tips:

A year ago – all six friends broke into the house; maybe they went as a dare to see if it was haunted.

Why two were left behind – the four chose those two to stay so that they could escape; possibly the two went missing and they did search for them but had to leave.

What it might sound like –

Donnie: 'I had the dream again. They were back.'

Sarah: 'How can they be? I mean, it was a year ago, right? No one can still be alive after a year in that house.'

Donnie: 'Maybe they're not alive.'

Sarah: 'Are you saying they're ghosts?'

How your group will help:

Directors will create clever ways of making this 'talking' scene interesting for the audience.

Acting Coaches will help create characters and relationships which will hold the audience's interest.

Peer Assessment:

How have other Storytellers delivered their plot?

Consider:

a) Are reasons clear for entering the house?

b) Is the haunting clearly explained?

c) Is exposition clearly explained?

Rate each section on a scale from 1 to 5; be ready to give reasons for rating it this way.

Shadowfall

Character Development	
Effect	
ARC	
Physical	

What you will learn ★★

To understand that the way a **CHARACTER** reacts to another shows the audience their relationship.

What you need to know...

To guide your group to producing realistic performances of a scene about four friends.

You will be looking at the way the four characters react to each other.

Even when someone isn't talking they can show what they think by the way they look, their body language and their mannerisms.

Make sure you know what each character thinks of the others and how you might show the audience that relationship.

What you need to do:

- You are going to take the friends and create good relationships between them. How does one character feel about another? Why?
- Then, you will need to help the actors show their feelings to the audience – all through reactions. That way the audience will be able to tell what each character thinks of the other.
- Make it clear through reactions what one character thinks of another.

Ideas to help you:

Hints and Tips:

Some reactions to think about:
Facially:
- one raised eyebrow (or both!)
- looking at, or away, from someone.

Vocally:
- small laugh only the audience hears
- tutting under their breath.

Body language:
- folding their arms
- leaning towards a character.

Distance:
- turning their body away deliberately
- stepping towards another character.

How your group will help:

Storytellers will create the story of why the characters have survived.

Directors will make the scene move quickly and keep the audience's interest.

Peer Assessment:

How have other Acting Coaches delivered a character arc?

Consider:
a) Can you easily identify the relationship between each character?

b) Is a range of physical skills used to communicate relationships or only one or two from the list given above?

c) Is a range of emotions shown with these relationships?

   Rate each section on a scale from 1 to 5; be ready to give reasons for your rating.

Acting Coach Acting Coach Acting Coach Acting Coach Acting Coach Coach 3.2

Shadowfall

Director Director Director **D** 3.2

What you will learn ★★

To use **MOTIVATED MOVEMENT** to keep a talking scene 'alive' for the audience.

What you need to know...

To lead your team in creating a scene where a group of friends gather together and plan out what they are going to do.

This is going to be a very 'talky' scene which will need clever directing to make sure the audience's interest is held.

You will need to find different reasons why characters move around the stage and make it look natural as well.

What you need to do:

- Direct your Storyteller's scene so that the characters don't just stand around talking. The point of this scene is to allow the audience to understand the story. The dialogue will help but your job is to make it more than a radio play!
- Think about different reasons for moving a character, so that the audience can follow the events but feel interested.
- *Remember – make the moves natural.*

Ideas to help you:

Hints and Tips:

Reasons to move a character:
- They get a drink.
- They switch the TV off or on.
- They look at a newspaper.
- Cooking is a great excuse to have a character move around.
- Eating – especially picky food, and regular visits to the table.

Any of these ideas can help you move a character and keep the audience interested.

How your group will help:

Storytellers will create a scene where the story is explained to the audience.

Acting Coaches will help create characters and relationships that the audience can relate to.

Peer Assessment:

How have other Directors delivered their staging?

Consider:

a) How much movement is actually used in this scene? Is the scene static (people standing still most of the time) or are characters moving around?

b) Do the movements have a purpose? (E.g. Do they move to emphasise a speech? To emphasise a relationship?)

c) Does the staging consider the audience so actors don't 'block' each other?

Rate each section on a scale from 1 to 5 and be ready to give your reasons for rating it this way.

Shadowfall

What you will learn ★★

To understand how a 'FLASHBACK' scene can help explain the background to your characters.

What you need to know...

To create a scene for your group which takes place the previous year.

That means you will need to think about how the characters would have once reacted to each other.

Try and create a difference, a contrast.

The more the audience understands about the characters, the more they will care for them.

What you need to do:

- Think of a scene which shows all six characters a year ago.
- You will need to think of how the relationships have changed in a year.
- You will also need a point to the scene. What does it tell us about the overall story?
- This is your chance to show the audience something of the characters' backgrounds.
- Why are the two missing? Why might some of the four feel guilty?
- Try and explain some of the story from a year ago, but not so much that the audience doesn't need to see the rest!

Ideas to help you:

Hints and Tips:

Relationships

- Two characters could have been friends before and now, a year later, they blame each other.
- One character may feel obsessed with finding out what happened to the two missing friends.

Point of the scene

- To let the audience realise how dangerous the house is.

How your group will help:

Directors will stage the scene so that the audience is clear when it is taking place.

Acting Coaches will provide a history for the characters, so the audience can learn something about them.

Example 👓

Keshia wanted to show that it was entering a specific room that trapped the friends. She built in a twist to this idea by having the characters argue about which room to enter. The four characters made fun of the two for being scared to join them. This is ironic because the two are never seen again!

Storyteller Storyteller Storyteller ⑤ 3.3

Unit 3

Shadowfall

What you will learn ★★

To understand how to play the same character from a different point in their life. How then to make this clear to the audience.

What you need to know...

To lead your actors in creating a scene that shows all six characters from a moment one year ago.

You will need to think what might have changed in that time.

One of the main things will be their relationships.

Some will get on better or worse with others.

That can be a useful contrast to show the audience.

What you need to do:

- Help your actors think about different ways of playing the same characters from a year ago.
- You will need to think about body language, costume (clothes), language and especially relationships.
- In one year a person can change who they like and why they like them. Make use of this fact and try and show a contrast in a few of the relationships.
- The point of the scene will be to let the audience see what changes have happened for these characters and what they have lost in addition to their two friends.

Ideas to help you:

Hints and Tips:

- A character may be more immature a year ago.
- A character may be less confident a year ago.
- You can show different reactions to characters (see Session 2).
- This is a good opportunity to show the audience what kind of people the two missing 'ghosts' are.

How your group will help:

Storytellers will create the scene set a year ago which allows the audience to see what happened then.

Directors will create the staging so that the audience know that this scene takes place a year ago.

Example 👓

Lianne decides to have all the actors wear something different. They use different slang – saying 'cool' instead of 'wicked'.

She also decides that two of the characters may have liked each other a year ago, so she asks them to look at each other in a way that the audience can see their attraction.

Finally, she decides that one of the characters giggles a lot more a year ago because they are less mature.

Unit 3

1 2 **3** 4 5 6
Session

Shadowfall

Audience Awareness
Impact
STAGING
Tension

What you will learn ★★

To understand that staging can help an audience realise **WHEN** a scene is taking place.

What you need to know...

To lead your group in staging a scene that is a 'flashback' to another time.

A 'flashback' is when the audience sees something from the past. You will be finding ways of making it clear to the audience that this isn't the same time period as the previous scenes.

The clearer it is, the clearer the audience will be as to what is happening in the overall story.

What you need to do:

- Decide how you will show the audience that this is a 'flashback'.

- You can use lights, sound, costume, etc. Make sure your cast know when this scene takes place – a year before.

- How will you change from the previous scene to this one? And then changing to the next scene is just as important.

- The audience can be told by the words the actors speak, but you can help by making the whole stage and movement different.

Ideas to help you:

Hints and Tips:

- Different clothes.
- Change the lights (blue is used a lot for flashbacks).
- Use old songs.
- A freeze-frame, like a photograph, begins and ends the scene.

You can use any combination of these ideas.

How your group will help:

Storytellers will create the detail of the flashback.

Acting Coaches will help the actors perform their characters a year younger.

Example 👓

Vicky decides to have the lights go down and the sound of paper tearing begins. The actors move into the flashback scene and then the lights come up. The sound stops and the cast are lit with one single light from the side.

At the end of the scene the cast freeze and the modern-day lights return.

Shadowfall

Stimulus Stimulus Stimulus Stimulus **3.4**

What you will learn ★★

To understand the theme for your 'Shadowfall' drama so that you can begin to create an effective ending.

This session...

In this session you will create a scene which shows the four surviving friends entering the house in their search for their missing mates. Perform as much of this scene in silence, to help create tension and to focus the audience's attention on how the characters interact.

Also you will use this scene as a way of showing your audience what your play is about. Your play is obviously a scary play, but what is it about? Remember, in the Sophie Smithson unit how your play was about social responsibility? So, now ask yourself what it is that your play is about – guilt and how people deal with it perhaps?

What to do next:

● Decide as a group what your play is about – this is called the theme.
● Now look at your area below and see how you can help show that to your buddy group.

S STORYTELLER

You need to create a scene that shows the audience the friends entering the house AND shows elements of your play's theme.

The characters need to show their relationships here. If you make these clear, even in a silent scene like this, the audience can see some of the theme your story is telling.

For example, if two people have just had an argument but going into the house one puts their hand on the other's shoulder... Well, that's friendship as a theme!

C ACTING COACH

You need to help the actors show the reality of the haunted house situation.

If the actors play it for real then the audience are more likely to believe it!

This is not easy to do, especially when not many people have been in a haunted house. The way actors do this is to play the 'reality of the moment' – thinking about what it would really be like in that situation and how they would react if it were for real.

D DIRECTOR

You need to direct the Storytellers' ideas to gain the most tension you can for the audience.

Contrast is a great way to create tension – slow movements followed by something fast can easily make people jump!

Contrast can also be a change in atmosphere or lights, sound or emotion.

Alter anything and the audience will notice – so do it for effect!

What you will learn ★★

To understand the theme for your 'Shadowfall' drama so that you can begin to create an effective ending.

Assessment

Ⓢ STORYTELLER

Assessment: INTENTION

- Think of scary things that could happen when they enter the house... lights on in strange places, moving pictures, closing doors... all subtle and suggestive.

- See how many ways you can carefully show the theme of your play in this scene.

Ⓒ ACTING COACH

Assessment: EFFECT

- Make sure your actors play what the characters would really feel – not too brave! It's easy to want to make your character look really impressive but not so effective for the audience.

- Look for a range of different reactions – you don't want everyone being scared or worried in exactly the same way. The audience likes to see contrast, remember!

Ⓓ DIRECTOR

Assessment: TENSION

- Direct your actors so that they move in a way that seems real to the audience. They aren't really breaking into a house, but their slow and quiet movements have to make the audience think they are.

- Think what sounds you want to use in a house to create tension – a ticking clock, a squeaking door, etc.

- Remember – you are also looking to show the theme in this scene. If, for example, it's friendship, then show how the friends react to each other as they enter the house (they may not get on, but then friends don't always!).

Finally – once you've chosen a theme and rehearsed the scene, show the whole play so far (all four scenes) to your buddy group. Let them Review your work so you can Respond.

Unit 3

1 2 3 **4** 5 6
Session

Shadowfall

3.4

Review Review Review

What you will learn ★★

To understand the theme for your 'Shadowfall' drama so that you can begin to create an effective ending.

Now you have created the first half of your 'Shadowfall' story, how do you want to affect the audience at the end? Watch your buddy group perform their work so far but review the work done by your counterpart: Storytellers review Storytellers, etc.

The idea is to help/advise them while they advise/help you.

S STORYTELLER

- Does the opening scene make you want to watch more? ☐
- Does the 'exposition' make the story clear? ☐
- Does the flashback tell you about the characters' backgrounds? ☐

C ACTING COACH

- Are characters shown clearly physically? ☐
- Do reactions show the characters' relationships? ☐
- Have characters shown their age through different physical actions? ☐

D DIRECTOR

- Is there a strong 'hook' at the start of the story? ☐
- Does the character movement keep your interest? ☐
- Is it clear that the flashback is from the past? ☐

(If you have been given 3 ticks you have successfully achieved your assignment!)

What do you think your buddy group's play is about? (Guilt, friendship, responsibility, etc.)

Now tell your buddy group what you think their play is about – do they agree?

Now that you have told your buddy group what you think their drama is about (what their theme is), which scene do you think they need to work on most to show the theme more clearly?
What can they change to help show the theme?

What was the best part of your buddy group's drama so far?

Always give reasons for your opinions!

Think about the theme of your buddy's play. What kind of ending might there be with a story like this? Suggest ideas to your buddy group for their final scenes.

What you will learn ★★

To understand the theme of your 'Shadowfall' drama so that you can begin to create an effective ending.

Now you have reviewed your work with the help of your 'buddy group', you need to respond to these comments and work out what you must keep in mind as you now work towards an ending.

You are going to create your own drama soon which aims to scare the audience. So...

Look at your area of responsibility. Which 'concerns' are likely to be important to you as you create your own drama, given what your buddy said:

S STORYTELLER

CONCERNS

- Making the first scene memorable and scary ☐
- Explaining the plot using exposition in a clever and interesting way ☐
- Using a flashback to show the characters' backgrounds to the audience ☐

C ACTING COACH

CONCERNS

- Use physical performance to show character ☐
- Encourage more reactions to show character and relations ☐
- Have actors 'play the moment' to create realistic emotions ☐

D DIRECTOR

CONCERNS

- Having a strong impact on the audience at the start ☐
- Using good movement to keep the audience interested in a talking scene ☐
- An effectively staged flashback that shows the audience your characters at a different time ☐

Your 'Shadowfall' story should scare the audience but have your buddy group suggested anything else you might be saying with your story (e.g. making the audience think about guilt, or fear or friendship)?

You now need to change some earlier scenes to show this theme – e.g., have your main character feel even more guilty, needing help to overcome his feelings – this would make the story much more about how people deal with guilt. How might you change some of your earlier scenes to make sure they focus even more on your chosen theme?

What do your Storytellers, Acting Coaches and Directors need to do now to finish the story?
Think about your theme and where that might lead the play. What do you want to leave the audience thinking and feeling?

Shadowfall

Storyteller Storyteller Storyteller S 3.5

What you will learn ★★

To understand that a moral dilemma for the characters can create strong **CONFLICT** for the audience.

What you need to know...

To lead your group in creating a scene that has the four friends meeting with their two 'lost' friends and having to make a difficult choice.

The audience hear that only four people can leave the house. This will lead to conflict for the characters and, if you can make the audience care about all six, then they will not want anyone to stay behind.

The result? Tension for the audience!

What you need to do:

- Create a scene where the four friends find the 'ghosts' of their two lost friends. The two lost friends explain that only four people can leave the house. Now that all six are back together the group have to decide which two are to stay behind.

- You need to create as much emotional tension as you can. Characters could blame each other or themselves.

- The audience should be wondering who is going to sacrifice themselves to let the others escape.

- The choice you make here will depend on what kind of story you want – sad, happy, scary, etc.

- Choose the right characters to stay and the audience will feel what you want them to!

Ideas to help you:

Hints and Tips:

- A year ago they made the same choice and left two behind. Would they do the same now or have they changed as people?

- Do you have two characters volunteer to sacrifice themselves?

- If you were in this position, what would you really do? Drop hints to the audience about what the two friends have suffered in the year they've been trapped.

- What if the two 'ghost' friends aren't telling the truth? What if they want all four other friends to stay and there is no escape? See how many different ways you could end this story.

How your group will help:

Directors will make the scene full of emotion through movement.

Acting Coaches will give the actors the motives for why they choose what they do.

Example 👓

Alice worked to make the audience feel sorry for the two ghosts, by using 'half references' (a statement that is deliberately never finished) to suggest the ghosts have been tormented in various ways.

This makes the audience feel sorry for them, since it makes them imagine what the torment could be.

Shadowfall

What you will learn ★★

To understand that scenes of high emotion still need to have a **RANGE AND CONTRAST** to the way actors perform.

What you need to know...

To lead your group in performing their characters with a whole range of emotions.

This scene is full of emotion but you want the audience to follow it and not grow tired. For this, you will need to encourage your actors to have *range*. This means that they don't just shout, or cry, all the time.

They find different ways of being emotional.

This keeps the audience interested and caring about the characters throughout the scene.

What you need to do:

- Help the performers act out their characters in a big decision full of tension and emotion.
- Actors will need to find a range to their performances – if the scene is just a lot of shouting the audience will get bored.
- Your job will be to plot out the 'highs' and 'lows' or the ebb and flow of the scene. When do the arguments become very heated and when are there moments of quiet thoughtfulness?
- Mixing these moments in performance creates wonderful tension for the characters and the audience!

Ideas to help you:

Hints and Tips:

- Sometimes gentle laughter can be a sign that someone is sad and has given up!
- How close an actor is to another character will show what they are thinking.
- Remember to have your actors focus and play the reality of the moment (see Session 4). If they believe, the audience will.
- Eye contact is very important in these scenes.
- Underplaying an emotion is a very powerful way of affecting the audience.
- Less is more, as the saying goes!

How your group will help:

Storytellers will create the climatic scene where the characters have to choose who stays.

Directors will make the scene have as much tension through staging as they can.

Example 👓

Vicky asked her group who felt guilty for leaving their friends. The one with least guilt sat and chatted quite innocently.

This showed to the audience how guilty they all felt by their distance from the two ghostly characters.

Shadowfall

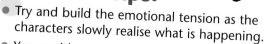
What you will learn ★★

To understand that tension can come from emotions as well as physical actions. And that a good story climax should have emotional **TENSION** for the audience.

What you need to know...

To lead your group in producing a scene that has the audience rooting for your characters.

How you place characters on the stage – *the staging* – will affect how much tension the audience feels.

How close one character is to another is very important. But also where a character needs to move to or from affects how much tension the audience feels.

What you need to do:

- Direct a scene where the four friends discover their remaining two 'ghost' friends in a single room. In this room they learn that the house expects two people to stay. They have to decide which two friends are going to remain behind.
- How would you stage this? Four friends on one side of the stage with their 'lost' friends on the other?
- Would you have a place, or object, that holds the captured two people?

Ideas to help you:

Hints and Tips:

- Try and build the emotional tension as the characters slowly realise what is happening.
- You could create even more tension by creating a time limit – they have to decide within five minutes or the house takes them all!

How your group will help:

Storytellers will create the scene where the characters decide who is to stay.

Acting Coaches will help the actors create conflict in the way they react to those choices.

Example 👓

Carly decides to have a camera on a tripod. This camera is pointing at the two 'lost' friends when the four others enter the room.

The camera, the audience will believe, is somehow freezing the two friends in place. So, when the four finally move forward, the audience feels tension at what is going to happen when they stand in front of the camera.

Shadowfall

What you will learn ★★

Create an ending that fits the theme and Overall Objective of the story you are telling the audience.

In this session...

You will create an ending to your play. Once the characters have decided who is to stay behind, what happens next? Do we see them leave the house? Do you show the remaining four characters another year later? Do you add a twist? Do you end with a smile?

The ending of a play is how you 'wrap it up'. The ending is what the audience is left with after the tensest moment (the climax). It gives them chance to think about what's happened and what it means. This makes the ending extremely important.

What to do next:

- Think about the theme of your play that you decided in Session 4.
- With this theme in mind, what effect do you want to have on the audience? For example, if your play was about friendship, do you want the audience to be left thinking just how much friends will do for each other? If so, then you could have a friend sacrifice themselves so the rest of the group can escape.

 STORYTELLER

Think about the feelings you want to leave the audience with. From this you should be able to tell what kind of ending you want to have.

If they're meant to be happy, then in the ending you could show the characters meeting a year later, relieved at the choice they made. If it's unhappy, you could have all the characters struggling to escape the house as the lights fade...

Choose a mood and then choose an ending!

C ACTING COACH

The ending is your chance to wrap up the characters' arcs.

Where did each start the play as a character? How can you show that they've moved on and grown? In what way can the audience see how the events have changed them?

Think about relationships and reactions at every stage, showing how they have changed too.

With events as traumatic as these, anyone would have changed. Think how to show the audience this.

D DIRECTOR

Make sure you have agreed the mood of the ending with the Storytellers. Once you have that, you can create the atmosphere and energy that you need to.

Usually an ending will have a contrasting mood to the climax.

Think about speed of movement, blocking and energy on stage for this contrast.

The climax will be full of tension so an ending is more of a release.

Unit 3

Shadowfall

Assessment 3.6

What you will learn ★★

Create an ending which fits the theme and Overall Objective of the story you are telling the audience.

Assessment

S STORYTELLER

Assessment: **INTENTION**

- A final scene does not have to be long. It just needs to send the signal to the audience that the play is over and this is what you want them to think about.
- You could leave the audience with a twist, if you wanted. The last scene changing something they thought they knew into something totally different.
- A final scene is a great way of showing more of your chosen theme.

C ACTING COACH

Assessment: **ARC**

- The more you can encourage your actors to show emotions they haven't displayed before in this final scene, then the more rounded their characters will seem to the audience.
- The more emotions a character shows, with good reasons for them all, then the more they will affect the audience and make them believe.
- Remember – have them 'play the moment'!

D DIRECTOR

Assessment: **IMPACT**

- If the climax is fast, then make the ending gentle and slow so that the audience get to catch their breath.
- See if you can have the ending contain some tension, even if it's not the same as the climax. You still want the audience interested until the very end.
- Try and create a final image which will stay in the audience's mind – the way people stand, the props and lights – can make a vivid picture for the audience.

Remember, once you have arrived at your Overall Objective (the message you want to convey and the audience reaction you want) all decisions must be driven by it.

What you will learn ★★

Create an ending which fits the theme and Overall Objective of the story you are telling the audience.

Now you have created the final scene to this drama, share all your work with your 'buddy group'.

Watch them perform their work and review the work of your counterpart (Storytellers review Storytellers, etc.)

The idea is to help/advise them while they advise/help you.

S STORYTELLER

- What feelings are you left with by the story at the beginning and end? ☐
- Is the Overall Objective shown? ☐
- Does the climax of the scene keep you tense? ☐

C ACTING COACH

- Are characters' motives obvious? ☐
- Do actors show good contrast? ☐
- Are physical skills used to show subtle reactions? ☐

D DIRECTOR

- Is non-naturalistic staging used well to tell the story? ☐
- Is the staging used well to keep your interest? ☐
- Does the contrast in energy keep you watching the play throughout? ☐

(If you have been given 3 ticks you have successfully achieved your assignment!)

> Write in this box what you believed was the Overall Objective for your buddy group.
>
> Now show it to your buddy group. Discuss how near (or far!) you were – and why!

> What was the best part of your buddy group's drama? Give reasons for your opinions.

> Which part showed their Overall Objective most clearly? Give your reasons.

> Which part needed to show the Overall Objective more clearly? Suggest improvements.

> How might they develop this drama further? Where could they go with it next?

Shadowfall

What you will learn ★★
Create an ending which fits the theme and Overall Objective of the story you are telling the audience.

Now you have reviewed your work with the help of your 'buddy group', you need to respond to these comments and work out what you must keep in mind as you now think about your group's own version of 'Shadowfall'.

You are going to create a drama now which provokes a reaction from the audience. So...

Look at your area of responsibility. Which 'concerns' are likely to be important to you as you create your own drama from now on, given what your buddy said:

S STORYTELLER
CONCERNS

- What intention do you need for each scene in order to achieve your Overall Objective?
- How will the intention arise out of the ideas you've had?
- What conflicts occur to drive the story on and are they appropriate?
- What causes conflict for the characters?
- How does the plot provoke reactions from the audience?

C ACTING COACH
CONCERNS

- What sort of effect should each actor try to create with their character?
- How will motives help create this effect? How will they be shown?
- What character arcs are needed and how will they be shown?
- How can character be shown rather than always being told?
- Are the characters different from each other?

D DIRECTOR
CONCERNS

- What sort of opening impact is your Overall Objective going to need?
- How can you provoke the right reaction at the end of the play?
- What will your set be like in order to maximise your staging?
- How will the staging contribute to your Overall Objective?
- How will tension be built up to a climax at the end?

Think about the overall purpose of this drama – your Overall Objective. What reactions do you want to provoke from the audience? These will help you create your Overall Objective.

What ideas have you had that might help you achieve this Overall Objective?

Good luck, as you now start to devise your own drama with these things in mind!

Shadowfall

Characters: Robert, Lorna, Ben, Paul, Marie, Helen.

Scene One

In the darkness we hear the sounds of photographs being flicked. As the lights slowly come up, with low ominous music playing in the background, we see ROBERT sat on his bed. ROBERT is looking at a bunch of photographs and shaking his head every so often. He stops when he reaches the end and throws all the photos onto the floor, burying his head in his hands.

As soon as he does this, a light comes on behind him revealing PAUL and MARIE standing glaring at him. The light goes out and ROBERT hasn't noticed. He rubs his face and picks up one of the photos. The light behind him comes up again and the figures of PAUL and MARIE are several steps closer to ROBERT. He still doesn't notice them.

This happens once more, leaving PAUL and MARIE standing right behind ROBERT, just as he is about to turn around, having picked up the photos. He turns, jumps at seeing them both.

PAUL and MARIE speak at the same time, just as ROBERT turns to face them.

Paul & Marie: **You left us!**

They both reach out to ROBERT's face as though to dig into his eyes. The lights cut out quickly and in the darkness we hear loud music start to play.

Suddenly the music cuts out.

We see ROBERT sit up in bed, the photos falling to the floor. He is breathing fast and looking terrified. It takes a moment for him to realise that it was a dream. He relaxes when he understands. The music fades out and he is breathing normally.

The phone rings and he jumps again.

Robert: *[answering it, scared]* **Yes? Who is it? What... what d'you want?**

A light comes up on the other side of the stage and we see LORNA in bed, photos on the floor by her side. She looks like she's had a terrible dream as well.

Lorna: **I had that dream again.**

Robert: **Yeah. Same here.**

Lorna: **So did Ben and Helen.**

Two more lights, on separate beds, come up on different parts of the stage. BEN is sitting up, HELEN is on her back running her hands through her hair. Both look like they've had bad dreams.

Robert: *[nodding]* **Right. OK. I guess we can't put this off any longer.**

Lorna: **I was hoping you'd say that.**

Robert: *[gathering strength]* **Let's meet up in the morning. Can you let Ben and Helen know?**

D Directors – the audience will be in the dark, hearing noises they can't identify...
This is our staging hook! (Session 1)

S Storytellers – the audience gets its first fright here, hooking them in when PAUL and MARIE suddenly move closer...
This is our story hook. (Session 1)

C Acting Coaches – Robert needs to convince the audience he is scared for quite a while but he relaxes when he hears Lorna speak, showing the audience what he thinks of her. (Sessions 1 and 2)

Lorna: I already did.

PAUL and MARIE's lights go out.

Robert: *[laughing]* You're amazing, did you know that?

Lorna: *[smiles]* Yes. But thanks for saying.

Robert: See you in the morning.

Lorna: Sleep well.

Robert: And you.

He turns off the phone and kisses it, just as LORNA does the same. LORNA's light goes out. ROBERT is sat on his own. He looks at the photos again and lies back on the bed. The lights fade to blackout.

Paul & Marie: *[whispered in the darkness]* You left us!

Scene Two

ROBERT and LORNA are outside the haunted house. The house is set back and up a long drive, but is still visible at the top of the road. ROBERT and LORNA have backpacks on and are waiting. ROBERT is putting a video camera in his bag.

Lorna: Where did you put the other tape?

Robert: The one we recorded tonight? *[she nods]* I left it in my bedroom. *[puts on a scary voice]* If anything happens to us now, they've got a record of what we're doing and where we went.

Lorna: Thanks, you really know how to cheer me up.

BEN comes running into the scene, looking angry. HELEN is a few steps behind.

Ben: What the hell are you two doing?

ROBERT looks at LORNA before answering BEN.

Robert: What we said earlier, Ben. You were there. You said your piece on the tape.

Ben: I didn't know you meant we were coming tonight! You've got to be kidding, right? You're going in now? Lorna just texted me to tell me *[he points at LORNA]*. I thought you were joking earlier. I thought we were doing some kind of tribute to them both. *[He pauses]* You really want to go in, don't you? What a waste of time.

Lorna: *[gently]* If it's such a waste of time why are you here?

There is a pause between them all. ROBERT looks down at the floor and HELEN puts her hand on BEN's arm.

Ben: *[giving way a little]* I didn't want you messing up again.

Robert: It's still my fault, is it? Was it just me that left them or maybe – hey, here's a thought – were there another three people nearby who also deserted them?

Ben: The whole thing was your idea last year. Just like now.

S By setting this scene just outside the house we help the characters tell the audience what has happened and why they're doing this… in other words, we have clear exposition! (Session 2)

D There is a lot of talking in this scene. It's all needed to explain to the audience what is happening, but your job will be to make the characters move and react enough to keep the audience interested throughout.

(Session 2)

S storyteller **C** acting coach **D** director

Lorna: Ben, don't. There's no need for this. You're either backing us up tonight or you're heading home. Which is it?

There is another pause and HELEN looks to BEN, shocked when he doesn't answer.

Helen: Ben? Tell them. Tell them we're not staying. Tell them what you said to me on the way up here.

BEN looks at HELEN and then looks at the house, unable to speak.

Helen: He said... *[Suddenly nervous]* He said that there was no way you were going to drag him inside there again.

Lorna: I don't remember anyone dragging him inside last year. He seemed pretty damn happy to me.

Helen: You forced him! He would have been on his own otherwise.

Lorna: Are you serious? 'On his own'? How old is he? He didn't have to come, did he?

Helen: *[frustrated]* Come on, Ben, tell them.

Robert: Yeah, 'mate', tell us.

Ben: *[reluctantly]* I'll come.

Helen: What? No. Ben, no. You said... No, you can't do this. What've you just been telling me? Why do this? It's nearly midnight, for crying out loud!

Ben: I'm sorry, Helen, I really am. But... *[he shrugs]*

Robert: *[finishing for him]* They're your friends. And any chance there's something we can find out, then we need to do it.

Ben: *[looking at him for the first time in a while]* Yeah. Something like that.

Lorna: Good for you, Ben.

Helen: No, not good for you! Am I the only one with a brain tonight?

Robert: Calm, Helen, we don't want to wake the neighbours, do we?

Helen: Yes, I damn well do if it means we'll stay away from that place.

Robert: Marie was your friend, Helen. Don't you care what happ...

Ben: Hold on, Robert, that's not fair.

Helen: *[to ROBERT]* Not care? Me? You know what I've been through since they disappeared. You know how difficult it was for me. Marie was my best friend, like Paul was yours. At least I showed some emotion over her.

ROBERT looks at HELEN and then shakes his head, shouldering his bag and walks upstage to the gates of the house.

Robert: Do what you want to, Helen. I guess it's all choices, isn't it? Like leaving them there last year. That was all *our* choice. This – *[he points at the house]* Well, this one's mine. Make it yours if you want to, but don't tell me how to feel.

C Helen's line of 'You forced him' is a weak argument. But, it shows how desperate she is to stop them going in to the house again. This shows her relationship to Ben and her reactions to heading back into the house. (Session 2)

Helen: *[after a pause]* **Look, Robert, I'm sorry.**

Robert: *[turning to her]* **Yeah, so am I.**

Helen: **I know you care but... That place. It scares me. I still have nightmares about it, you know.**

Lorna: **About them? Paul and Marie?** *[HELEN nods]* **So do we. You know that. That's why we're all here. I want to find out what happened to them, sure. But I also want to stop the nightmares from getting worse.**

Ben: **Amen to that.**

Robert: **So, we're agreed?**

They look at each other. BEN and HELEN exchange a glance and HELEN looks away, not sure how to nod.

Ben: *[turning back to them both]* **I haven't got a torch. I reckon it's going to be dark in there again.**

ROBERT grins and delves into his backpack, producing two torches.

Robert: **I brought spares just in case.**

Ben: **'In case' we came along?**

Robert: **Maybe.** *[He smiles and then looks back up to the house]* **It's definitely going to be dark, though.**

Lorna: **Can we put this off a little longer or do we have to go in now?**

Ben: **Now. Before I change my mind.**

Helen: **I'd be happy if you did.**

Ben: **You don't have to come.**

Helen: **And leave you on your own? Sure. Like that's going to happen.**

HELEN reaches out her hand and BEN takes it. ROBERT raises his eyebrows to LORNA and heads up the path to the house. BEN and HELEN head off. LORNA looks after the three of them and takes a deep breath.

Lorna: *[speaking to herself]* **Come into my parlour, said the spider to the fly. Oh, hell, déjà vu, all over again.**

With a shrug she heads off and begins the journey to the house.

C The moment when Helen and Robert apologise shows another side to both their characters, as they both recognise how scared they are. It is worth playing this moment quietly and letting their friendship come through to the audience. (Session 2)

D This last line from Lorna should make the audience worry about what is going to happen next. This keeps them interested but also sets up for the flashback scene next... (Session 3)

S storyteller   **C** acting coach   **D** director

Scene Three

We see MARIE holding a video camera and pointing it at PAUL. PAUL is grinning wildly, looking full of energy and fun.

Robert: And, action!

Paul: Alright, couch-potatoes... Here's the info-dump: We are here. You ain't. We'll have this video as proof that we stayed the night. That'll win us some fame, fortune and lots of girls!

Robert: *[stepping into the camera line]* It's the only chance he's got.

Paul: Ah, shove it where the camera can't see, Robbo.

Marie: Hey, you two geeks, get packed, we're heading out in a minute. You can talk to your 'fans' when we get back.

Paul: *[moving to her side quickly]* Ooh! But what if...?

Robert: *[moving to her other side]* – we don't ever come back!

They both make scary movie soundtrack sounds either side of MARIE.

Marie: *[pause]* Oh, dear God, shoot me now. Just get ready, you two.

Paul: *[pretending to be a young boy]* Yes, miss!

MARIE starts to exit when LORNA comes into the room, nodding to the lads.

Lorna: What are those two up to?

Marie: *[looking at the two lads as they fiddle with the video camera]* Boys with toys. Paul still wants to try and record tonight for school. *[LORNA is about to speak when MARIE holds up her hands]* Don't ask, I don't know. I think he wants to prove something. You know, that he's not a loser, that he can do something.

Lorna: So he's going to make a documentary of us breaking into a haunted house?

Helen: *[coming into the room]* I wish you wouldn't say that. Remind me why I'm doing this again.

Ben: *[also entering]* Because your wonderful boyfriend asked you to.

Helen: You are so going to owe me big time for this.

Ben: *[grinning at LORNA and MARIE]* Don't I know it.

Paul: *[looking over at the four of them]* Right, we're done. Come on you lot. We're ready.

Lorna: For what?

Robert: We're going to record a message from all of us. We've got the start already. Come on, lovers – get yourselves over here.

BEN drags HELEN over to where ROBERT and PAUL are standing. ROBERT is behind the camera making final adjustments.

Ben: OK. What do we do?

Paul: *[pointing]* Stand there. We'll group round you.

LORNA and MARIE look at each other and sigh, then move over.

D In this scene there is no clear signal to the audience that this is a flashback. How are you going to make it clear to the audience? Different lights, sound, staging? You choose! (Session 3)

S Notice that the idea for the video recording runs through the entire play and has a 'twist' ending. This helps the audience think they know what is happening until the very end...

C This scene is a gift for Paul and Marie as it gives the actors a chance to show the audience a lighter, funnier side to their characters. (Session 3)

S storyteller **C** acting coach **D** director

Marie: Where do you want us?

Robert: *[grinning]* Now you're asking.

Lorna: Grow up.

Paul: In a few years' time, maybe. But until then – I'm young and I intend to live forever! *[sees how unimpressed they are and sighs]* Right, stand there.

Everyone moves into position and PAUL nods at ROBERT who turns the camera 'on' and then moves next to the other five as the camera is rolling.

Paul: *[waving at the camera stupidly]* Hey, again, everyone.

There's a pause and PAUL encourages the rest of the group to say 'Hi'. Reluctantly, they do so.

Paul: Great. Thanks for that enthusiasm. *[back to the camera now]* Well, we're here because… Hey, Marie, why are we here?

Marie: Me? *[he nods at her and she blinks in embarrassment suddenly not so confident]* Um… We've… er… Well, Paul's wanted to do this for a while and it's his choice for the weekend thing.

Paul: Yeah, and it's got to be better than Helen's walk in the park last weekend.

Helen: It was a great park! All those animals. The flowers.

Robert: Exactly! Not my idea of fun. Haunted house? Now there's a way to spend a weekend.

Marie: So, the gang is heading into the house tonight and Paul wants to record it so that he can get some money from… What's that programme called?

Paul: 'Most Haunted.' You really don't know anything, do you?

Marie: *[ignoring his barb]* So, we're making this in the hope we'll get some serious money when we break into the house illegally and then find it's full of dust and all other really 'interesting' stuff.

Robert: All right, cut, cut, cut!

Paul: Yeah, thanks, Marie. You could have taken it seriously, you know.

Lorna: Come on, you three, stop arguing, let's head out.

PAUL and ROBERT look at each other and grin, nodding as they load the camera into the bag and gather the other four together.

Paul: Alright, let's go and make history.

Marie: Oh, please, you are so going to be the death of me. Just lead on.

They all exit, ad-libbing as they go.

C The lines about who chooses what happens each weekend need to be made clear to the audience so that they understand what is happening. (Session 2)

S storyteller   **C** acting coach   **D** director

Shadowfall

Scene Four

We are in a deserted, empty and dusty house. We can see a couple of clocks on a mantelpiece. Suddenly a light comes through from one side of the stage and moves around the set. After a pause, ROBERT enters the room through the window. He is breathing fast and has a torch in his hand. The torchlight strikes different objects in the room. The room looks like a living room, with books, easy chairs and a fireplace.

ROBERT steps in slowly, trying not to make a noise. Behind him, looking cautious but excited, is BEN. BEN grins at ROBERT and reaches off-stage, through the 'window', to HELEN. HELEN does not look at all happy, but takes a breath and climbs through the window. She has a torch as well and shines it erratically around the room, not moving from where she is standing.

Finally, LORNA jumps up onto the window ledge and perches there, looking around with her own torch. She watches the others and then nudges HELEN with her foot, to ask her to move out of the way. HELEN jumps and then moves. LORNA slides down onto the floor and starts to speak.

Lorna: **I'd forgotten what a dum...**

Her words are cut off by the other three saying 'sshh' at her. She shrugs her shoulders and mimes zipping her mouth closed.

ROBERT takes a breath and moves into the room. As he passes the fireplace, there is a small glimmer of light which suddenly sparks up in it. HELEN is the only one to notice and she doesn't say anything as she stands staring at it. BEN ignores her and moves to the bookcase. He pulls a few books from the shelves and blows dust from them, using his torch to read and then discard them.

Without warning the window suddenly slams shut. All jump and HELEN gives out a small cry, stifling it herself before the others can say anything. Seconds later the door on the opposite side of the stage swings open. There is light coming from the room within.

All four people are breathing heavily now.

Robert: *[whispered]* **Paul?**

There is no reply. BEN is by the fireplace now and jumps a mile when it suddenly lights up. We can hear the roar of a fire, but it sounds distorted. The sound dies down and then the fire flickers to life. Everyone's head has turned to it.

BEN mimes that he didn't do anything. LORNA rolls her eyes, trying to make a joke of it but she is beginning to be scared herself. The tall lamp she is standing by suddenly comes on with a loud click.

We can hear the four of them breathing loudly now. At the window the darkness that was outside suddenly changes. There is a sunrise judging by the way the light changes and the room becomes lit. The four move to the window and look out.

Helen: **It's still midnight. Why is the sun out?**

D Remember contrast here... You are moving from the past to the present, from a funny, happy scene to scene four where the house should be spooky and the characters suddenly scared. Contrasts throughout! (Session 4)

C Remember that this scene has hardly any speaking in it. Your characters, therefore, need to be communicated to the audience through face and body language. This needs to be realistic, so play the moment to convince the audience. (Session 4)

S Making the audience wonder what is going to happen next makes them worry for the characters. Think what other events can take place which worry the audience. (Session 5)

As soon as they reach the window a musical box on the fireplace comes alive and plays some music. The four are now reacting almost as one, turning from one event to another. HELEN reaches for BEN's hand and he grabs her by the arm. ROBERT taps his torch on his chin, thinking, and looks around the room.

ROBERT moves from window, to lamp, to fireplace – still burning happily, to the bookshelves, now brightly lit from the sunlight. The following dialogue is spoken very quietly and controlled.

Ben: **Rob, let's go, mate. Please.**

Robert: **Yeah. You don't have to ask me twice. Back the way we came.**

LORNA is by the window and tries to open it. It won't budge.

Lorna: **Someone's already thought of that.**

They look at each other as the sun fades down and they are left with their torches on. The lamp goes out and the fire smoulders and fades.

There is a pause and then the sound of footsteps from the other side of the door. The four friends look to each other and huddle together. The footsteps approach and there, in the doorway, is PAUL. He is dressed in the same clothes as before, but looks like he did in the very first scene – serious, unsmiling and scary.

PAUL tilts his head, as though pointing to the room he has just come from. He smiles a sickly smile, then turns and walks back the way he's come.

LORNA looks at her friends and gestures that she will go alone and they should stay. HELEN grabs her arm and shakes her head violently. ROBERT takes a breath and raises both eyebrows as if to say 'ah well, all together, then'.

ROBERT leads the way, the torch lights bobbing around as the four friends follow where PAUL has gone.

Scene Five

PAUL and MARIE are sitting at a big dining table. They both turn their heads as the other four friends enter the dining room. When they speak their voices are different from in scene three – somehow more flat, threatening and full of lifelessness.

Paul: **Hey, gang.**

Marie: **You made it.**

Paul: *[standing and beginning to move towards them]* **At last.**

Marie: **We thought you'd forgotten about us.**

Paul: **And we couldn't have that, could we?**

The four, ROBERT at the front, LORNA, HELEN and BEN behind, stand there unsure of themselves. The lights are a sickly colour and the music is low and worrying.

Robert: *[scared and trying not to show it]* **It's good to see you both.**

C Here's another example of playing the moment… Think how scared you would actually be if all of these things started to happen around you. That makes it easier to act!
(Session 4)

D The rhythm of events, how they build up to Paul entering the room, is crucial for this scene. It builds to Paul's entrance, so be sure to have things happen slowly first and then climax here.
(Session 4)

 S storyteller   **C** acting coach   **D** director

Paul: *[still moving forward, towards the four of them]* **Really? Took you long enough, though, didn't it?**

Lorna: **Where've you been all this time?**

Marie: *[moving to the clock away from the group]* **Here. All this time.**

There is a pause. The tension mounts as everyone stops.

Helen: **Why don't you just leave here? We were waiting for you, Marie.**

Marie: **Were you? I'm touched. We're both really touched.**

Ben: **The police came. They looked round. They didn't find anything.**

Paul: **It wasn't them we were waiting for.**

Marie: **It wasn't them who should have come looking for us.**

Paul & Marie: **Was it?**

Another silence falls. ROBERT steps forward to speak, trying to get closer to PAUL.

Robert: **We didn't know what had happened. Our parents. They wouldn't let us come back.**

Paul: **We're only your friends, aren't we? Not that important.**

Helen: **We didn't say that! That's not it. We've been thinking about you all year.**

Paul: *[stunned]* **Year? It's been a whole year?**

PAUL and MARIE look at each other and seem shocked. MARIE now looks even angrier. She turns back to the other four.

Marie: **You left us for a whole year?**

Robert: **It doesn't seem like a year to you?**

Paul: **We've been looked after.**

Ben: **What do you mean 'looked after'?**

MARIE gestures to the table. There is food there. It is steaming.

Helen: **I don't understand. It's food.**

Paul: **From where? We don't leave the house. Whenever we're hungry we just come into this room and the food is here. Waiting.**

Marie: **Waiting for us. But we never see who's made it.**

Paul: **Or what.**

LORNA moves over to the table and MARIE and PAUL move out of her way. LORNA reaches out and tastes the food. She likes it, reacts surprised and nods.

Lorna: **You've had this all year?**

Paul: **Yes.**

Marie: **You'll get used to it.**

S In plotting this type of scene you should be making the audience feel uncomfortable. After all, they know the four have left the two behind. Their emotions will be mixed, therefore, so they will be riveted to see what happens next. (Session 5)

C Paul and Marie need to be different here than from scene one or scene three. This should be their most scary, so leave room for that range to be seen by the audience. (Session 5)

S storyteller   **C** acting coach   **D** director

Helen:	What do you mean? We're not staying, Marie. We're getting you out of here.
Paul:	No. It doesn't work like that.
Marie:	We can't leave. And neither can all of you.

There is a small pause. Then ROBERT gives an uncertain laugh.

Robert:	What? We can't leave? We'll just go back the way we've come, thank you very much.
Marie:	No you won't. You can't. It won't let you.
Paul:	The house won't let you. But it's ok. It doesn't want all of you. Just two more. It's not greedy.
Ben:	You're joking. You must be. The 'house' wants two more of us. Why?
Paul:	It doesn't tell us. Just that it does. We've tried to go against it before but...
Marie:	*[they both look scared now]* But... we won't try again.
Paul:	Two of you can go. Two have to stay. That's the price of breaking in here. You can decide who it is to be.
Lorna:	How are we meant to decide that? *[looks up to the house as though talking to it]* How can you expect us to do that?
Marie:	If it's difficult, we have been given permission to choose for you.
Robert:	They'll find us. Our families. The police. I left a tape. A video tape in my room. They'll see it and know we're here. Then they'll come find us.

PAUL and MARIE both laugh.

Paul:	I did a tape. What difference did that make?
Marie:	So. Two of you can stay. Maybe more.
Paul:	Who's it going to be?

ROBERT, BEN, HELEN and LORNA all look at each other, reacting, not wanting to speak first. MARIE and PAUL smile, waiting patiently, as the lights dim.

D These moments here should be a shock for the audience as well as the characters. How can you make them more full of emotional tension? (Session 5)

S storyteller acting coach director

Scene Six

We see ROBERT leaning forward and switching on the camera. He grins and waves.

Robert: Hey guys.

LORNA, HELEN and BEN step into shot.

Lorna: It's the one year anniversary.

Ben: Paul...

Helen: ...And Marie...

Ben & Helen: ...Here's to you.

All four of them raise cans of coke in honour, clinking them together.

Helen: I feel a bit silly. Why are we doing this again?

Robert: Paul would have done this for us. We have to go back to see what's happened to them. This can be our journal.

Ben: Really? You'd do that? I thought you'd given up on them.

Robert: Nope. You up for joining us?

Ben: Yeah. Sure. Any day. Count me in.

Helen: I'm not going back there. Ever. You wouldn't see me dead in that place.

Robert: Lorna?

Lorna: *[grabbing his arm]* Someone's got to keep you out of trouble.

Robert: OK. So, we'll go looking. See what we find.

Lorna: To our friends, then...

ROBERT, LORNA, BEN and HELEN raise their glasses and call out to the camera.

All: To Paul and Marie.

Robert: *[quietly]* Wherever you may be.

The four of them freeze as though the tape has finished. All four locked into the final pose, glasses raised, ROBERT with a sad smile on his face.

There is the sound of static growing louder as the lights fade out. This crosses over until the static sound is loud and deafening and the lights are off completely.

Then the sound fades and the stage is left in silence.

The End...?

D Another contrast! The audience will expect to be frightened at the start of scene six, but you make them uncertain by creating lots of energy at the beginning of the scene to throw them.
(Session 6)

S See how the themes of friendship are linked here in the final scene. The video camera footage takes us back in time, leaving the audience wondering what happened in the end.
(Session 6)

C This last line of Robert's should make the audience feel sympathetic towards him. What has happened? they will think. This line should be played as 'sweetly' as possible.
(Session 6)

 S storyteller **C** acting coach **D** director

The Choice

Synopsis

Imagine a future where there are no waiting lists at the doctors. No waiting lists at the hospital. You receive all treatment free and immediately.

Sound far-fetched? Not if the government introduced the NHS Card for everyone!

This unit imagines that the government did exactly that – every person in the country is given an NHS Card for their birthday. Whenever they are ill, people take their NHS Card along to the doctors and get immediate treatment.

Sounds great? Yes…except, once you've used your NHS Card you won't get another one until your next birthday. You can only go to the doctors once a year, in other words. If you happen to be ill more than once? Well, that's the Choice you have to make…. How ill do you have to be to use that NHS Card up for the whole year? What if a friend or family member hasn't got a Card and needs yours? Would you give it up? Sell it?

This unit looks at these types of moral questions. The unit puts your characters in difficult situations and asks the audience – what would you do if you were faced with this same Choice?

Having characters facing difficult choices is what good drama is all about!

The Choice Unit Outline

SESSION FLOWCHART

S STORYTELLER

Session 1
Using 'resonance' to create an emotional impact on the audience

Session 2
To use conflict between characters to create tension for the audience

Session 3
Using non-naturalistic methods to show a character's background

Session 4
Using a montage sequence to show the passage of time

Session 5
To continue to develop characters that the audience can relate to

Session 6
Using the play's Overall Objective to help choose the ending

C ACTING COACH

Session 1
Having contrasting characters can engage an audience's interest

Session 2
Using the build up of reactions to create tension for the audience

Session 3
Showing a character's mind using non-naturalistic performances

Session 4
To show the audience how a character ages physically

Session 5
To show a character's decisions through their physical reactions

Session 6
Underplaying reactions to create the maximum effect on the audience

D DIRECTOR

Session 1
How to use contrast to create an emotional impact on the audience

Session 2
Using rhythm to create tension in a scene

Session 3
How to use non-naturalistic staging to tell a story

Session 4
Using staging to show the passage of time

Session 5
Using cross-cutting to create tension in a scene

Session 6
To use props and symbols to create an emotional impact on the audience

With this unit we aim to link all aspects of the teaching in the past five years of our students' drama lives. This is no small feat! We give our students ownership of a simple but powerful moral dilemma and then ask them to populate that world with the right story, the right characters and the right climax to make the most out of the dramatic potential.

In order to achieve this, students are going to have to draw on storytelling, structure, tension, characterisation, research and strong emotional performances. Because of this demand 'The Choice' remains one of our most popular units by far. Students rise to the challenge as they can identify with all parts of the story at some level. This is strong stuff and the students relish every moment!

Ideas for introducing this unit to the students... Our first lesson with our pupils usually asks them to form a group of five or six characters. These characters are then invited to a public meeting where either an MP or a GP (depending on your preference) speaks to the whole class, who are sat in their groups of friends and family. This group has to vote on the new proposal for the NHS Card. It is not too difficult to sway a whole class into voting in the new system – especially if the 'only one Card a year can be used' bit of information is missed out! Once the group has voted for the system you can take the class forward a few years, to when the NHS Card system is in place. You can play a short scene at the doctors where one of them finds out they can't get treatment because they've used their Card already. The outcry this prompts is a good springboard for Citizenship issues as well as the unit as a whole!

Notes for consideration:

Safety warning: It's clear from the basic concept that 'The Choice' involves a lot of emotional work for the students. Almost every student we have ever taught has a connection to someone in an extreme health situation. We always warn students beforehand about the nature of the unit and allow them a 'safe' environment in which to work. We do not present ourselves as counsellors and would advise that this is the same for anyone reading this. However, students are remarkably resilient and without exception those pupils in these situations feel almost driven to tell a story about 'The Choice' that they face. There is something inexpressibly humbling in seeing a student create a moment in a play such as 'The Choice' that is so personal to them. Be aware, though, that students will try this and just be prepared so that you know how to handle it.

Resonance is one of the main driving forces behind this unit. For us resonance is when a character, a scene or event 'connects' with the audience. It is something the audience sees or hears which they can relate to in their own lives. The more moments, characters or situations students can employ in a drama; the more likely the audience will be affected in the intended way. An engaged audience is likely a moved audience.

Research: This unit works wonders for students in appreciating the value of research. If they are ill, how do the symptoms present themselves? If they are a doctor, how does a GP speak when with a patient? These are just two simple examples of how 'The Choice' lends itself to the seriousness and necessity for research. Once students own their story, it is easy to encourage them to research and use their research in performance.

Playing the moment: This is a phrase we use with our students to encourage them to think realistically about the situation their characters are in. Too often we have had times when a character is meant to be angered by another, resulting in virtually no response. 'Playing the moment' is used to have pupils think about what a character wants or is feeling and how they can express it. The three word shorthand is useful after this is explained!

The Choice Unit Outline

The Script: The script here has been written with a deliberate avoidance of any particular illness. For this script to be accessible by many schools, we felt it important to turn away from the minutiae of the illness and focus on the basic concept in the unit – namely, the choice faced by the characters.

There is no clearer unit in this book for consolidating learning about Overall Objective, either. A look at this script will show an attempt to move away from the 'easy' downbeat ending to a more uplifting ending. The effect on the audience is paramount in every scene with 'The Choice' and it's easy for students to see why. Most students will want the audience to cry by the end of their performance – and they quickly see how they can move the audience to that aim with every scene. Here we are trying to present an ending that may well bring a tear but not for depressing reasons!

It can also, as we have explained in the Introduction to this book, be used as a Scripted Performance in AQA's GCSE course. We have tried to build in moments that will provide a chance for actors to stretch their acting muscles. It can, of course, be added to or changed, in whatever way is needed.

Peer and Self Assessment Opportunities: (Sessions 2, 4 and 6)

In two of the Sessions (4 and 6) there are explicit assessments shown. Activities are provided that encourage buddy assessment – as described in the previous units.

The buddy system, as before, encourages students to look at each other's work. In this unit it is focused on Overall Objective and how that impacts on the audience. Who better to assess this than a small audience of your peers? The frames for these assessments can be found in the pages of the sessions that follow.

These Review Frames also have opportunities for students to use the learning they have covered to set themselves targets for next time they take on that leadership role.

By making this final unit so resonant – in a way that everyone can connect to on some level – students have no trouble committing to the work. It is, without doubt, our most successful unit and one that the students talk about, and debate, for a long time afterwards. Because the unit uses so much of the students' own personal ideas, the unit is its own motivation.

The Choice Unit Outline

A Look into the Future...

This unit of work looks at a possible future. You all know what it's like waiting at the doctors for treatment. Maybe some of you have been at the hospital for hours before anyone has even asked your name! So, imagine that some government in the near future found a way of making all waiting times disappear. When you want to see the doctor, go to the hospital or have an operation – you can!
All you need to do is have your NHS Card ready and you will be seen straightaway.

Sounds simple, doesn't it? But, the one thing the government doesn't tell you, until it's too late, is that this new NHS Card can only be used once a year. If you've used it already then you can't go to the doctors again. Not until your new NHS Card arrives on your next birthday.

So... there you are, with a few months to go before your birthday and you break your wrist. Do you use your NHS Card up by having the hospital put a bandage on it? Do you treat yourself because you don't want to use your NHS Card up on something so small when you might need it for something much more important?

And, what if someone in your family, or a friend, needed an NHS Card... Would you give them yours? How much do you love them?

Perhaps now you can see why this unit is called 'The Choice'!

What will you need to do?

STORYTELLER (S)

You will shape your story so that:
- The audience can understand and connect to your characters by seeing things they recognise from their own lives.
- To show the audience how characters' lives are changed over the course of a year.
- The ending of the story is carefully chosen to match the feelings you want to leave the audience with when they finish watching.

ACTING COACH (C)

You will lead your group in developing characters who:
- Show a range of different personalities for the audience to connect with at least one of them.
- Are performed with a whole spread of reactions so that the audience can see what they are thinking and feeling without the need for words.
- Can be performed with great subtlety to make them more realistic for the audience to respond to effectively.

DIRECTOR (D)

You will guide your group to affecting the audience in the following ways:
- Having a strong emotional impact by using tension, rhythm and the passage of time.
- To show how staging can be used to let the audience see inside characters' minds.
- How an overall emotional effect can be achieved by knowing where you're heading.

Production Outline

Session 1: Creating an emotional impact on the audience
This session needs to make the audience care straightaway. You will need to choose a central character that is able to get the audience on their side from this opening scene. This character needs to be ill yet not seem too weak. Not an easy task! You will then need to think what kinds of characters this person would have around them as friends and family.

Session 2: Showing how conflict creates tension
So the main character is ill. That means everyone is sympathetic, doesn't it? Well, not if you want some drama in your play! If everyone always gets on, then there would never be any tension. You now need to find possible ways and reasons for the surrounding characters to have differing opinions about the main character. Have the audience want to see how it's all going to end!

Session 3: Look inside your character's mind...
We can hear what someone says and we can see what they might be feeling. But, what if we could look into a character's mind, hear their thoughts about what is going on in their life? How much would the audience feel a connection, then? In this session we look at ways of showing the inside of a character's mind!

Session 4: One year in five minutes
How can you show the passage of nearly a year on stage? You can't glue the audience to their seats for twelve months, so you will need to squeeze time together. In this session you will learn about showing how a long time passes for the characters, but only a short time goes by for the audience. They will watch the characters grow and change and feel more connection with them.

Session 5: The Choice itself
We've introduced the problem; we've seen the characters and looked into their minds. Then we've seen how they deal with the problem over a period of time. Now, our main character faces a simple dilemma – a choice… the choice... of the whole play. Will they try and help themselves at the risk of a friend, or will they step back and let the illness run its course?

Session 6: The ending
Will it be a happy ending? Will the main character be cured? What happens to everyone else?
This session looks at the characters later in their lives and gets you to ask what might happen to them. How will you know? By deciding how you want to affect the audience. The Overall Objective which you and your group decide is essential here!

The Script: The Choice
Mark is a person who seems to have it all… Fit enough to try and run a marathon, with a girlfriend he adores and friends who he appreciates. Suddenly he finds he has an illness but no NHS Card. Yet he hasn't been ill this year. What will happen to him? Where has his NHS Card gone? Why is he reluctant to seek help?

Unit 4 The Choice
Narrative Menu

You may want to look at some of these story ideas to help you create your own version:

BLACK MARKET

If the NHS Card started to cause problems in the country, it wouldn't take long before a black market in Cards became active. There might be a small corner shop that pretends to be normal but actually sells 'fake' Cards, or a bloke you know down the pub who sells Cards to anyone with enough money.

You could create a play about this, using characters that don't like the black market but are forced to go against their morals in order to get treatment.

MORAL DILEMMA

The NHS Card gives you plenty of opportunities to create moral dilemmas (difficult choices) for your characters…

What if one person robbed someone else of an NHS Card just to help their friend? Is that fair and would the person accept the Card?

What if you knew someone received treatment but didn't have a Card. What would you do?
If they were a friend, would you turn them in or ask them how they managed it?

THICKER THAN WATER

Would you help a family member if you had your NHS Card but they had already used theirs up?
What if you didn't like that member of the family but someone closer to you asked you to give up your Card as a favour to them?

You could use this basic idea to explore what it's like to have family pressures on a person and a group of characters. If there was a friend and a family member who needed your Card, which person would you give it to?

TURNING TO CRIME

Doctors might end up working for extra money. You may be able to imagine a situation where a doctor is offered a few thousand pounds to work on a patient, even though that patient no longer has an NHS Card.

Would this cause problems for the doctor? What kind of situation would this lead the doctor into if someone found out? Blackmail is a possibility here and the pressures that the doctor finds him/herself in.

DESPERATE MEASURES

How far would you go to help someone you loved? If they desperately needed an NHS Card for treatment, what would you do? You could turn to crime, get friends involved, or even try and go for political change or use the newspapers.

This kind of action takes a very brave person. If that person started the play as very quiet and shy, but was forced to take action, you can tell the story of how they gain the confidence to become a braver person and tackle authority.

The Choice Narrative Menu

GUILTY PARTY

Imagine it's ten years after the NHS Card is introduced. People, who needn't have died, have passed away because they had no NHS Card. What kind of guilt would that make the politicians feel? What if you were the politician, or the doctor, who first thought up the idea and you were now looking back on the whole scheme after it had fallen apart and people had died needlessly.

ACCIDENTAL HERO

What do paramedics do in an accident? Do they have to check the casualties to see if they have an NHS Card on them before treating them? What if there was a paramedic who broke the rules and treated everyone they came across, even if they didn't have an NHS Card? Would they get caught? How do they feel, live and get away with it?

SCOOP

What if you were a newspaper reporter and you heard about something like the start of the NHS Card system? You may have overheard some politicians talk about it and then heard that there was a catch in the system (you can only use it once a year!). What would you do with that information? What might the government do if they found out you knew – would you be safe?

This kind of story can lead to a strong thriller-like piece which shows the responsibility of an individual for the world they live in.

ONLY WHEN I LAUGH

This story can be played for comedy quite easily. Imagine that you have an NHS Card but lose it. What kind of chain of events might have you go looking for it? You could come across a whole host of other characters who try and help you find it.

At the end of the story you could reach the doctors only to find out that there's nothing wrong with you after all!

Be careful – even in a comedy you need to create characters that are fully rounded and have as much of an emotional range as you can manage.

Written Coursework

Option 1

Write your own script for 'The Choice'. The basic idea of 'The Choice' – namely that you can only receive medical treatment once a year – is so simple that it offers many possible storylines that you might wish to develop.

Your teacher will be able to tell you if you are using our script, creating a story of your own (known as improvising) or using elements from a number of scripts plus your own ideas (called devising).

To help you create a basic storyline for your own version of 'The Choice' we have included some ideas before this page. These ideas are not the only ones! We're sure you can think of more, and better. However, they may help you come up with some ideas that really help you along. The choice is yours!

Option 2

Write a 'Response' – as in AQA's GCSE Drama Part 1.

This assessed work involves you comparing the ideas you have for your drama with another play from another time or culture.

The point of a 'Response' is to help you see why you have made the choices in your play that you have. Most people can understand their own work much better when they think about another piece of work in comparison.

We suggest you compare 'The Choice' with another play called '*Whose Life is it Anyway?*' by Brian Clark.

Have a look at that play if you can. Your teacher may well suggest another play with a similar theme of health, friendship or loyalty. The point is that you compare. When you look at your chosen script, you can write about that play and your own and learn more about how to play your chosen character.

Option 3

Edexcel Portfolio. After completing all the sessions in this unit, write a description of what techniques you have used and learnt.

Remember – you will have to ask your fellow creators (Storytellers, Acting Coaches and Directors) for advice on all the things you have learnt. It is important you don't just write about the techniques you have learnt for your own role, but also for the whole unit.

A portfolio requires you to have followed several rehearsal techniques, such as hot-seating and marking the moment, in this unit. Your teacher will have taken you through these approaches.

In this portfolio you can write up what techniques you have learnt, how you have used them and where you think you will use them in creating your own version of 'The Choice'. This shows the examiner you understand the words you use and can see how the techniques would be used in any production.

Unit Review Frame – Storyteller

(S) Name _____ Class _____ Date _____

*In this unit I have been responsible for leading my group in creating the **Narrative Structure** of our drama. This means making the story have a strong emotional impact on the audience. I have learned:*

INTENTION: *(when you set out to create a story/drama with a message)*

1. (Session 1) I helped my group make the audience feel sorry for a character by:

2. (Session 6) I made sure our intention worked through the whole play to the end by:

CONFLICT: *(finding ways to show differences in opinion, motives, attitudes and the way they affect the story)*

3. (Session 2) I helped create characters with different opinions and beliefs by:

4. (Session 5) I helped create the climax of the story where characters faced a choice by:

PLOT: *(how you structure or shape a drama to make a point)*

5. (Session 3) I have shown the audience inside a character's mind by:

6. (Session 4) I helped create the scene showing six months of the characters' lives by:

The thing that I am most pleased I have achieved is:

Next time I take on the Storyteller role I am going to try to improve:

Unit Review Frame – Acting Coach

(C) Name `_____` Class `_____` Date `_____`

*In this unit I have been responsible for leading my group in **Character Development**. I have helped them create characters with whom the audience can relate and feel emotional about. I have learned:*

EFFECT: *(when you set out to affect how and why the audience relates to the character)*

1. (Session 1) I helped my group create immediately sympathetic characters by:

2. (Session 6) I helped my group develop characters that made the audience care by:

ARC: *(showing the growth of a character, from before the story to its climax)*

3. (Session 4) Where I showed a character ageing using 'montages' by:

PHYSICAL: *(the skills you use to communicate your character to the audience)*

4. (Session 2) Giving motives to characters so they had reason for conflict – I learned:

5. (Session 4) Having characters show what was inside their minds by:

6. (Session 5) Creating tension between characters by a range of reactions such as:

The thing that I am most pleased I have achieved is:

Next time I take on the Acting Coach role I am going to try to improve:

Unit Review Frame – Director

(D) **Name** ----------------------------------- **Class** -------------- **Date** --------------

*In this unit I have been responsible for leading my group in developing **Audience Awareness** in our play. This has meant working to create a believable performance which affects the audience emotionally. I have learned:*

IMPACT: *(where you decide how you want your audience to react)*

1. (Session 1) Affecting the audience from the very opening scene by:

2. (Session 6) Making sure the ending has the emotional impact we wanted by:

STAGING: *(using the space onstage to communicate with the audience)*

3. (Session 3) I used staging to show the inside of a character's mind by:

4. (Session 4) I used staging to show how six months had passed in a montage by:

5. (Session 5) I used staging to decide on the best order of a scene by:

TENSION: *(creating situations that make your audience wonder what will happen next)*

6. (Session 2) I have used distance to help create tension by:

The thing that I am most pleased I have achieved is:

Next time I take on the Director role I am going to try to improve:

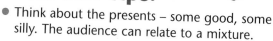
What you will learn ★★

To understand that 'RESONANCE' can be used to create an emotional effect for the audience.

What you need to know...

To create a short scene that makes the audience feel sorry for the main character.

An effective way of doing this is *resonance* – when you have a character do or say something that the audience can relate to.

An audience can feel resonance when they see or hear something that has happened to them.

This makes the audience feel a connection to the main character.

What you need to do:

- Create a scene where a group of friends are holding a surprise birthday party for the main character.
- At some point in the scene the main character comes in really upset. It turns out they have just been told that they have a serious illness.
- At this point the illness is not important – you are looking to make the audience relate to the main character, not think about the condition.
- Try and make the scene have little moments that the audience can relate to – have resonance with.

Ideas to help you:

Hints and Tips:

- Think about the presents – some good, some silly. The audience can relate to a mixture.
- Maybe make the main character not tell anyone what's wrong – that happens in everyone's life. More resonance!
- When the main character comes in you could have them make a cup of tea. Small actions like this are what we all do.

How your group will help:

Directors will be finding ways of making an emotional impact with contrasts.

Acting Coaches will be helping the actors create a range of characters for the scene.

Example 👓

Kerrie decides to have the scene set in a restaurant. Lorna isn't there. Her friends are ordering their food because Lorna is late and are complaining about her bad time-keeping (resonance!).

Then Lorna comes in and doesn't eat the food. Eventually Lorna tells them the news and everyone stops eating.

Acting Coach Acting Coach Acting Coach Acting Coach Acting Coach 4.1

What you will learn ★★

To understand that the right **CONTRAST** of characters in a play can help keep the audience interested.

What you need to know...

To lead your actors in creating a mixture of characters that have an intended effect on an audience.

In every story you need a range of characters – no one likes to watch a play with all the characters being unhappy all the time!

So, your job will be to make the character types varied in your group. This means that the audience is likely to have at least one person they can relate to themselves!

What you need to do:

- You will be looking at a range of characters to take part in your play. Your main character is going to become seriously ill – so it might help to have that character as bright and cheerful as possible at the start. That way the actor has a range to show during the play.

- What other people might be in that person's life? Can you make them varied, so that the audience can see different personalities?

- Also, think about how they are connected – friends, lovers, family, and work colleagues.

- As many different connections as you can make will help the audience see the characters as real.

Ideas to help you:

Hints and Tips:

Possible relationships include:
- boyfriend/girlfriend
- best friend
- brother/sister
- parents – biological, foster or step
- friend of the family
- ex-boyfriend/girlfriend.

Each of these can, of course, have whatever personality you want!

How your group will help:

Storytellers will create a scene where the main character reveals that they are ill.

Directors will be creating an impact using contrasts.

Example 👓

Mickel chooses to have the main character, Lorna, be an energetic and lively personality. There are two friends – one sarcastic, one loyal. There is also a boyfriend and an ex-boyfriend (which will probably help with some tension later on!).

Finally, there is an elder sister for Lorna, so that we get to see how Lorna reacts to her family.

This range means there is something in the group for the audience to relate to.

The Choice

What you will learn ★★

To understand how to use contrast to create an emotional **IMPACT** on the audience.

What you need to know...

You will lead your group to direct a scene which has a strong emotional impact on the audience.

One of the best ways is to use contrast. This can be in speed of movement – from fast to slow – from high energy to low, from happy to sad.

Whatever the change, the audience will be pulled along with it and their emotions with them!

What you need to do:

- Using the story that your Storyteller has created you are going to choose an impact you want to have on the audience.
- This impact could be sadness, shock or concern.
- Which character in your story is going to create this effect for your audience?
- Now decide how best to create the impact on the audience when they hear the news.
- Contrast is a change in action – from fast to slow, or movement to stillness.

Ideas to help you:

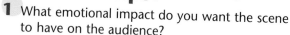

Hints and Tips:

1 What emotional impact do you want the scene to have on the audience?

2 Which character is going to help create that impact?

3 What contrasts can you use?

Some contrasts you could use:

- Have everyone stop moving when the main character tells them of their illness.
- Use sudden silence to add impact.
- Music used at a key moment.

Why not try combining some of these?

How your group will help:

Storytellers will create a scene where a character tells their friends and family they are ill.

Acting Coaches will create a mixture of characters to help the audience relate to the play.

Example 👓

Laura had the friends frantically putting together a project that had an urgent deadline. This required fast action around the stage. She had one character move much slower, which prompted the others to criticise him. He falls unconscious in the seat. The frantic actions suddenly stop when they realise this – a sudden change.

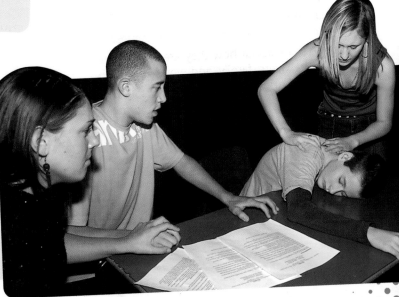

Storyteller Storyteller Storyteller S 4.2

What you will learn ★★

To see how **CONFLICT** between characters can be used to create tension for the audience.

What you need to know...

To create a scene for your group that has the main character revealing they cannot receive help for their illness.

This leads to conflict for the other characters – all of whom want the main character to get help, but not all of whom understand why they won't do so.

This conflict makes for gripping viewing for the audience!

What you need to do:

- Create a scene that follows on from the first. You will have the five characters react to the main character's news.
- This scene, though, has the main character revealing that they cannot use their NHS Card because they have already given it away.
- Remember – in this story a character can only get medical help with an NHS Card. If it's given away they have to wait until their next birthday before getting a new one!
- Think about how this news would come out. If your main character is pushed into explaining themselves, then there is more conflict!

Ideas to help you:

Hints and Tips:

Possible reactions:
- Some might become very quiet.
- Some might try denying it.
- Others might laugh, thinking it's a joke.
- The more cynical might just shrug their shoulders.
- Someone might want to sort the main character's life out.

Some, or all, of these reactions might build up to make the main character explain why they can't receive treatment.

How your group will help:

Directors will have the scene's rhythm worked out.

Acting Coaches will help by creating strong reactions to the main character's news.

Peer Assessment:

How have other Storytellers delivered their conflict?
Consider:
a) Is the reason clear why the main character cannot get treatment?
b) Is there some form of tension shown that comes from other characters having conflicting reactions?
c) Are the reasons for the other characters' reactions clear to the audience?

Rate each section on a scale from 1 to 5 and be ready to give your reasons for rating it this way.

What you will learn ★★

To understand that character **REACTIONS** can be used to create tension for the audience by building them up.

What you need to know...

To help your actors create a series of reactions that the Director can use to build tension. People don't just react in one way and then stop – we continue to react at all times.

The actor should show reactions to one piece of news and then react to how other characters are reacting as well! This build–up of reactions can be very useful in creating tension.

What you need to do:

- You are going to help your actors create a build–up of reactions.
- Each of the five support characters will need to decide how they are going to physically react to the main character's news.
- As each of the five react, you will need to encourage the actors to look at each other and react to those reactions.

  E.g., if one character is upset, it can lead to another character being even more upset.
- This is a build-up of reactions which your Director can control for maximum effect on the audience.
- The more choices you give your Director, the easier you make their job.

Ideas to help you:

Hints and Tips:

Some physical reactions to consider:

- A character may just widen their eyes.
- Two characters could then look at each other.
- Non-verbal communication (when nothing is said) is very powerful.
- Raised voices can force a character to become defensive.

Remember – all these reactions are for the audience's sake. Make sure they can see them clearly!

How your group will help:

Storytellers will make the story build.

Directors will have the scene's rhythm worked out.

Peer Assessment:

How have other Acting Coaches delivered physical skills?

Consider:

a) How easily can you explain each character's reaction to the news?

b) How many forms of non-verbal communication can you spot?

c) How clear is their relationship with the main character?

Rate each section on a scale from 1 to 5 and be ready to give your reasons for rating it this way.

What you will learn ★★
To understand how to use rhythm to create **TENSION** in a scene.

What you need to know...
To direct your Storyteller's scene in a way that builds to another revelation – namely, that the main character cannot receive treatment for their illness.

In order for this to reach a climax – the most dramatic point – you will need to look at the rhythm of the scene.

Rhythm is when the speed of events changes – in this case you could build up the rhythm faster and faster until the main character has to reveal the news about their card.

The audience is gripped by the rhythm and feels tension as a result.

What you need to do:
- Direct your Storyteller's scene so that the audience are swept along with the building pace of the moment.
- You should aim to finish the scene where the main character reveals they cannot receive treatment. At this point you can use contrast again (see Session 1) to affect the audience with this second news.
- The rhythm of a scene is not just the speed with which people speak, but the speed of events as well.
- Think what energy the scene needs to have at the most dramatic moment, and then how you can build up to that point from the start.

Ideas to help you:

Hints and Tips:
Ways of creating good rhythm:
- If you build up to a climax, always try and start with slow, quiet beginnings.
- Try and have the actors talk faster the more speed you want, but not so fast the audience doesn't understand what's being said!
- Intensity is also important. Someone can speak a line gently or with real passion – the more passion, the more speed you create in the audience's mind.

How your group will help:

Storytellers will create a scene using conflict to make the main character reveal their plight.

Acting Coaches will help by creating strong reactions to the main character's news.

Peer Assessment:
How have other Directors delivered this tension?

a) How well have they created a calm, slow start to the scene?

b) How does the scene increase in speed in order to reach a dramatic climax?

c) How clearly has the Director shown a range of emotions during the scene, perhaps even showing the emotions intensify?

Rate each section on a scale from 1 to 5 and be ready to give your reasons for rating it this way.

What you will learn ★★

To understand that characters' backgrounds can be shown using non-naturalistic methods.

What you need to know...

To create a scene that shows the audience each of the character's feelings.

This scene must use *non-naturalistic* elements.

This means that 'normal' ways of presenting the scene can be thrown out!

Non-naturalistic simply means ways we wouldn't normally see in the real world.

By doing this, you can show the audience straight into a character's mind.

What you need to do:

- Firstly, be clear what each of your six characters think and feel about the main character's illness.

- Once you have decided that, you can start to think of different ways of presenting that information to the audience.

- You will not be using non-naturalistic approaches just for the sake of it. Find a reason why an unreal approach to this information would be helpful to the audience. For example, showing every character reading from their diaries would let us see into their minds.

- The audience want to see into the characters' hearts and minds. Can you find a way of showing that?

Example

Rachael asked her group to get across their feelings using silence and non-verbal communication. She wanted to keep words to a minimum. This meant that when words were used, they had impact. Numerous physical actions were performed in a montage of events, such as everyone writing in diaries.

Ideas to help you:

Hints and Tips:

- Why can't the main character use their NHS Card? Who has it? Why?

- Do any of the support characters want to give their own NHS Card?

- If so, why…? If not, why not?

- How the NHS Card system works. Remember that the audience may not be familiar with the basic idea – you could use this scene to explain it to them, and how characters feel about it.

How your group will help:

Directors will stage the scene using non-naturalistic techniques.

Acting Coaches will help the actors perform in a non-naturalistic style.

Storyteller Storyteller Storyteller ⑤ 4.3

What you will learn ★★

To see that **NON-NATURALISTIC** performances can show an audience a lot about a character's thoughts and feelings.

What you need to know...

To lead your actors in deepening their characterisation through *non-naturalistic* means.

Non-naturalistic acting is presenting the character in a way that is not quite real – this may mean that you stand stiffly as your character speaks, or appear just as a voice, or record yourself on video!

This allows the audience to just see inside the character's mind and heart in a refreshing way.

What you need to do:

- Help your actors perform their characters in a way that allows the audience to see inside the character's mind.

- For example, if the scene asks for a character to explain how upset they are, then that actor could carry an over-large tissue.

- This is obviously not 'real' but lets the audience see what the character is thinking straightaway.

- Non-naturalistic theatre can be used as a shorthand way of showing the audience something about a character.

Ideas to help you:

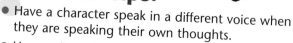

Hints and Tips:

- Have a character speak in a different voice when they are speaking their own thoughts.
- Use masks to hide the faces of the actors you don't want to be the main focus.
- Have repeated body movements rehearsed as though they are dance patterns.
- Costume could help you create the non-naturalistic effect you are after.

How your group will help:

Storytellers will create the scene with as many non-naturalistic elements as possible.

Directors will create the staging that makes the non-naturalistic ideas as developed as possible.

Example 👓

Dan decides to use props and make-up to help show the characters thoughts and feelings. The main character wears a burial suit; the other characters wear sad clown faces to show they are upset. The main character rides a broken bicycle to show the audience that they don't feel right!

What you will learn ★★

To see how non-naturalistic **STAGING** can be used to effectively continue a story for the audience.

What you need to know...

To lead your group in creating the staging for the Storyteller's scene.

This scene uses *non-naturalistic* ideas to get across characters' thoughts and feelings.

Your job is to make those non-naturalistic elements come alive on stage.

What you need to do:

- Decide how you will stage the Storyteller's scene. The scene is written using non-naturalistic ideas – things that don't happen in everyday life.

- Your job is to find a way of putting those ideas on stage so that the audience is interested in seeing something different even as they are learning about the characters.

- You can let your imagination run wild – so long as you can show the inside of the characters' minds you have no limits. Sometimes this can be scary!

Example 👓

Richard had the main character on a stretcher with the friends around him. Each character spoke no more than two sentences. As they did this the other characters whispered the words 'scared, worried,' repeatedly. After the final speech the characters suddenly look at each other in silence.

Ideas to help you:

Hints and Tips:

- All six could stand facing the audience, lit one at a time.
- All six could be writing in their diaries.
- A series of freeze-frames with different voice-overs.
- Characters could make comments as they move around the stage.
- The cast could act as a chorus for the action – speaking as one voice as a character explains their thoughts.

You can use any combination of these ideas.

How your group will help:

Storytellers will create the detail of the flashback.

Acting Coaches will help the actors perform their characters a year younger.

director Director Director Director **D** 4.3

163

Stimulus Stimulus Stimulus **4.4**

What you will learn ★★

To use a montage to show the audience how your characters develop over a number of months of story time.

This session...

You will create a scene which takes the audience through the next six months of the characters' lives. We see what happens to the main character as they begin to fall ill. What effect might this have on the other characters? What about their choice to hand over an NHS Card – should they do this or are they scared to do so? You will show all this by using a *montage*.

What are montages?

A montage is a collection of short mini-scenes which fit together to form a whole scene. You will show short scenes which show the characters over six months. A mini-scene can be as short as one word, one look or a small event. Try not to have too many, but pick out which moments are the most important for your character's arc and show reactions.

● Now create your montage using the roles below to help...

(S) STORYTELLER

Create a montage scene which shows the characters over a six–month period.

You could have the whole montage without speaking, or you could use music under all the action to help the mood you are after.

Which parts of the story you choose to tell in the montage is the most important decision you will make.

Don't show everything – just choose the most dramatic moments and link them together.

(C) ACTING COACH

Help the actors create more range to their characters in the montage.

A montage is a great opportunity to show the audience other sides to your character that they haven't seen yet.

A good character arc will show the audience one part of a character and then a reason for a change in that character.

(D) DIRECTOR

Direct the Storytellers' ideas for their montage so that the audience is clear that six months is passing.

It may be obvious to your group that you are showing six months pass by... But, the audience must be clear about this as well!

Think of different ways that you could show the passage of time.

What you will learn ★★

To use a montage to show the audience how your characters develop over a number of months of story time.

Assessment

S STORYTELLER

Assessment: **PLOT**

- Think about who the audience want to see in the montage. This will help make your choice about what can happen.
- Have a definite start and end in mind – maybe it's a month or an event that begins or ends it.
- Have a couple of simple stories going on at the same time – this keeps the audience totally hooked!

C ACTING COACH

Assessment: **ARC**

- Your main character will need to look and behave more and more ill, so some physical change will be needed for the audience to see.
- How the other characters change through the main character's illness is a good arc – some may try and accept what is happening and some turn away.
- Think carefully how you can show this to an audience and so make it clear what is happening.

D DIRECTOR

Assessment: **STAGING**

- You can use sound and music to show the passage of time – Christmas Carols being sung, then Happy New Year songs, to indicate just a week passing by, for example.
- You might have a character reading a series of books (moving from one to another) to show time.
- Having a character move slowly across the stage can help the audience see time go by.
- The lights could come on from one side of the stage and then the other.

Finally – once you've practised the montage, rehearse it and show the whole play so far (all four scenes!) to your buddy group. Let them Review your work so you can Respond.

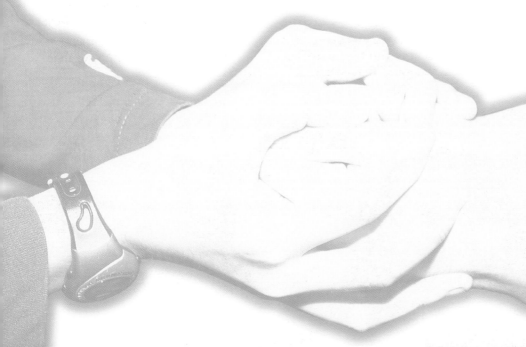

What you will learn ★★

To use a montage to show the audience how your characters develop over a number of months of story time.

Now you have created the first part of 'The Choice', how do you want to affect the audience by the end of the story? Watch the whole of your buddy group perform their work so far but only review the work done by your counterpart: Storytellers review Storytellers, etc.

The idea is to help/advise them while they advise/help you.

S) STORYTELLER

- Is there strong conflict in the story helping create tension? ☐
- Are backgrounds shown clearly through a non-naturalistic scene? ☐
- Does the montage scene have well-chosen character moments? ☐

C) ACTING COACH

- Are all the characters different enough from each other to keep your interest? ☐
- Do the characters' reactions build up? ☐
- Can you understand all of the characters' motives? ☐

D) DIRECTOR

- Is there an emotional impact at the start of the play? ☐
- Have the scenes used a good rhythm to create tension? ☐
- Is the non-naturalistic scene staged well? ☐

(If you have been given 3 ticks you have successfully achieved your assignment!)

What do you think your buddy group's play is about? (Guilt, friendship, responsibility, etc.)

Now tell your buddy group what you think their play is about – do they agree?

Now that you have told your buddy group what you think their drama is about (what their theme is), which scene do you think they need to work on most to show the theme more clearly? What can they change to help show the theme?

What was the best part of your buddy group's drama so far?

Always give reasons for your opinions!

Think about the theme of your buddy's play. What kind of ending might there be with a story like this? Suggest ideas to your buddy group for their final scenes.

What you will learn ★★

To use a montage to show the audience how your characters develop over a number of months of story time.

Now you have reviewed your work with the help of your 'buddy group', you need to respond to these comments and work out what you must keep in mind as you now create the rest of your drama.

You are going to create your own drama soon, which aims to affect the audience in some way. So...

Look at your area of responsibility. Which 'concerns' are likely to be important to you as you create your own drama, given what your buddy said:

S STORYTELLER

CONCERNS

- Having a strong emotional impact on the audience from the start ☐
- Having good character conflict to help create tension ☐
- Show the characters' backgrounds clearly ☐
- Choose effective moments for use in the montage scene that helps continue the story ☐

C ACTING COACH

CONCERNS

- Have characters that contrast with each other ☐
- Create a build-up of reactions so that the audience can understand what they are thinking ☐
- Physically perform the characters so that the audience can see what is happening inside their minds ☐
- Use the montage scene to show a range of emotions to all characters ☐

D DIRECTOR

CONCERNS

- Having a strong emotional impact on the audience from the start ☐
- To create tension by using contrast and rhythm in all scenes ☐
- Use non-naturalistic staging to show inside a character's mind ☐
- Effectively stage a montage so that the audience feels the passage of time ☐

'The Choice' story you create should affect the audience emotionally but have your buddy group suggested anything else you might be saying with your story (e.g. making the audience think about family, death or friendship)?

This is known as your theme.

You now need to change some earlier scenes to show this theme – e.g., have your main character feel even more afraid of death, trying not to talk about their situation – this would show them afraid of death. How might you change some of your earlier scenes to make sure they focus even more on your chosen theme?

What do your Storytellers, Acting Coaches and Directors need to do now to finish the story? Think about your theme and where that might lead the play. What do you want to leave the audience thinking and feeling?

Unit 4 The Choice

1 2 3 4 **5** 6
Session

What you will learn ★★

To understand that an audience will continue to sympathise with a character for as long as they understand them.

What you need to know:

To create a climatic scene for your group that pushes your characters to their limits!

This scene is six months down the line and the pressure has now built on all of them.

You still want the audience to sympathise with the characters but you need to have them understand all the actions and motivations.

The more you explain, the more desperate you can make a character and still have the audience on your side.

What you need to do:

- Create a scene which has the main character being very ill. There should be one support character that now begins to get desperate and pressure the others to give up their NHS Cards for the main character!

- In the end the main character will have to face the one who is pressurising everyone else.

- This scene needs a fine balance between the different motivations of all the characters. Make it clear to the audience why they choose to do what they do.

- Remember – if the characters say 'yes' to giving away their NHS Card, then there's no story! Find convincing reasons why most of them would say 'no'.

Ideas to help you:

Hints and Tips:

- Break the scene into three sections –
  1) see how ill the main character is;
  2) see how pressured the other characters feel;
  3) and the confrontation between the main character and the one doing the pressuring.
- Show why the main character wouldn't want the NHS Card from anyone.
- You can create extra tension for the audience by not fully explaining what the main character is going to do. Will they accept the NHS Card?

This is the emotional climax of the story, so make sure there is plenty of conflict.

How your group will help:

Directors will make the scene cut between the three elements.

Acting Coaches will give the actors the motives for why they choose what they do.

Example 👓

Kerrie had two of her group argue about why the other person should offer their NHS Card. She got one character (A) to really pressurise the other (B) who didn't seem to have a good reason not to offer it. The argument built up until B confessed in a dramatic way as to their real reason for needing to hold on to it.
This made A react guiltily.

Unit 4 The Choice

1 2 3 4 **5** 6
Session

Character Development
Effect
Arc
PHYSICAL

What you will learn ★★

To understand that a character's decisions can be shown in their **PHYSICAL** reactions, not just their dialogue.

What you need to know:

To help your actors portray their characters' decisions about a difficult problem.

Audiences will always look at an actor's face for a reaction – it is this part of being a viewer that we can use.

Have your actors make their decisions on their faces only.

Try and reduce the amount of dialogue they have to speak and see if they can communicate the decision with their face alone!

What you need to do:

- Help the actors create believable and varied reactions!

- In this scene all the characters will be making a choice. Four of them will be being pressured by a fifth to give up their NHS Card. The audience will need to see how they react to this pressure and the decision they make.

- This leads onto the final confrontation when the person pressuring offers the main character an NHS Card. How can you show the main character's reactions in this case? Shock, anger, gratefulness?

- Remember – be sure your actors know their characters. Why and how they react is very much a personal decision for each actor.

Example ◯◯

Laura decides to have exactly the same physical reaction to the decision-making from all four characters.

The characters will say 'no, I just can't' but use completely different tones of voice. They will each shake their heads but at different speeds, with different eye contact to show how they feel.

Ideas to help you:

Hints and Tips:

Possible reactions:
- Shake their head.
- Turn away, head bowed to show they are feeling shame.
- Raise their hands and back away from the one asking.
- Angrily knock the person asking out of the way.
- Hesitate, open their mouth to speak and then shake their head slightly.
- Ignore the person asking.

How your group will help:

Storytellers will create the climatic scene where the different characters are under pressure.

Directors will make the scene move from one part of the stage to another.

ting Coach Coach Acting Coach Coach **4.5**

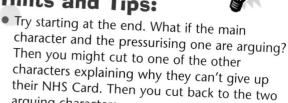
Director Director Director D 4.5

What you will learn ★★

To understand that cross-cutting can be an effective way of building emotional tension in the audience.

What you need to know...

To stage your Storyteller's scene in a way that helps the audience feel the pressure within the scene.

Cross-cutting is a drama method which allows you to show more than one perspective by moving forwards and backwards in time.

In this one scene you are going to find the best order of events so that the audience is left wanting to see what happens.

What you need to do:

- The scene you will be directing has three main parts to it –
  1) see how ill the main character is;
  2) see how pressured the other characters feel into giving up their NHS Card;
  3) the confrontation between the main character and the pressuring one.
- You will need to work out where each of these three elements would be best placed and how best to switch between them.
- Think about height, levels, sound, lights and music to make it clear you are cutting between different events.
- Make sure the audience understand the sequence.

Ideas to help you:

Hints and Tips:

- Try starting at the end. What if the main character and the pressurising one are arguing? Then you might cut to one of the other characters explaining why they can't give up their NHS Card. Then you cut back to the two arguing characters.
- If you placed the two arguing characters in the middle and had the other four characters around, stepping in for flashback scenes. That would mix the order of the events and keep the audience interested.

How your group will help:

Storytellers will create the scene where the different characters are under pressure.

Acting Coaches will help the actors create conflict in the way they react to those choices.

Example 👓

Dan has the main character in a hospital bed with his heart monitor beeping. Dan then cuts to two friends arguing over the NHS Card. Finally, Dan cuts back to the main character's girlfriend visiting him in hospital. The tension builds by seeing all sides of the story!

The Choice

What you will learn ★★

Create an ending which fits the theme and Overall Objective of the story you are telling the audience.

In this session...

You will create a final scene for your play. Remember (from 'Shadowfall') that a final scene is always a contrast with the climax. In 'The Choice's case, if the climax is full of heated emotion, then you will want the end scene to be quiet and considered. You will also need to carefully choose the mood and emotion you want to evoke in the audience.

The best way of doing this is imagining them all leaving your play – what do you want them to be doing? Crying? Laughing? Or a mixture?

What to do next:

● Choose how you want the audience to react to your play at the very end.

● This is your Overall Objective. Now you need to follow the guidelines below to achieve that ending.

S STORYTELLER

Choose an ending which fits the theme and the effect you want to have on the audience.

The ending is the last thing the audience will be left with from your play. So, make it count and see if you can make the audience feel what you want them to feel.

This ending must wrap up the storylines from the rest of the play – can you do that in a simple but strong way?

C ACTING COACH

To show your characters' emotions in as subtle a way as possible.

It is easy to be tempted into creating lots of emotion in your performance, especially in the last scene.

However, there is a phrase which is worth remembering:

LESS IS MORE!

This means that the less you overdo it, the more effect it can have on the audience's emotions.

See what subtle (small) ways you can affect the audience with your actors' performances.

D DIRECTOR

Create the final scene so that the audience is emotionally affected in the way you intend.

Think about your group's theme and Overall Objective. In other words, what do you want to say to the audience and how do you want to emotionally affect them?

You will need to think of ways of creating the right atmosphere and feelings for the audience. You can use sound, props, lights and sets to help with this.

Unit 4 The Choice

What you will learn ★★

Create an ending which fits the theme and Overall Objective of the story you are telling the audience.

Assessment

S STORYTELLER

Assessment: **INTENTION**

- The final scene needs to be one that looks at the main story and finishes it in a satisfying way for the audience.

- Think of what image you will leave them with. Do you want people left on stage, or an object to remind the audience of a character? These touches can stay in an audience's mind a very long time.

- It is always worth trying out two or three end scenes with your buddy group – let them see which one has the effect you want and then choose that one.

C ACTING COACH

Assessment: **EFFECT**

- Think about facial reactions – closing your eyes, raising an eyebrow or giving a small smile.

- Movement instead of words – such as lowering your shoulders, shaking your head instead of saying 'no', or raising your hands, etc.

- The speed you talk and the pauses you put between lines can carry a lot of emotion as well.

D DIRECTOR

Assessment: **IMPACT**

- You can choose a song to play over the final scene. Not so loud it interferes, but enough to help the audience know the mood of the scene.

- The lights can be set in a way that shows the feelings of the characters. Dark and sombre, or bright and cheerful, for example.

- Props – such as a photograph or jewellery can have meaning for characters which helps the audience relate to them emotionally.

Remember, once you have arrived at your Overall Objective (the message you want to convey and the reaction you want) all decisions must be made because of it.

What you will learn ★★

Create an ending that fits the theme and Overall Objective of the story you are telling the audience.

Now you have created the final scene to this drama, share all your work with your 'buddy group'.
Watch them perform their work and review the work of your counterpart (Storytellers review Storytellers, etc.)
The idea is to help/advise them while they advise/help you.

S STORYTELLER

- Is 'resonance' used well throughout the story to help you connect? ☐
- Does the character conflict seem real and full of tension? ☐
- Have the characters' actions made you feel emotionally affected? ☐

C ACTING COACH

- Can you tell a character's thoughts from their performance? ☐
- Do the characters show different emotions throughout the play? ☐
- Are the performances subtle and emotionally affecting you throughout? ☐

D DIRECTOR

- Is rhythm used well to create tension? ☐
- Do the group show the passage of time well in the montage? ☐
- Does the overall piece have a clear message and emotional impact on you, the audience? ☐

(If you have been given 3 ticks you have successfully achieved your assignment!)

Write in this box what you believed was the Overall Objective for your buddy group.

Now show it to your buddy group. Discuss how near (or far!) you were – and why!

What was the best part of your buddy group's drama? Give reasons for your opinions.

Which scene showed their Overall Objective most clearly? Give your reasons.

Which part needed to show the Overall Objective more clearly? Suggest improvements.

How might they develop this drama further? Where could they go with it next?

The Choice

What you will learn ★★

Create an ending that fits the theme and Overall Objective of the story you are telling the audience.

Now you have reviewed your work with the help of your 'buddy group', you need to respond to these comments and work out what you must keep in mind as you now start on your own version of 'The Choice'.

You are going to create a drama now which provokes a chosen reaction from the audience. So...

Look at your area of responsibility. Which 'concerns' are likely to be important to you as you create your own drama from now on, given what your buddy said:

S STORYTELLER

CONCERNS

- How do you want to affect the audience by the end of your play? ☐
- What effect do you need for each scene in order to achieve your Overall Objective? ☐
- What conflicts occur to drive the story on? ☐
- Are backgrounds clearly shown? ☐
- How does the plot provoke your chosen reactions from the audience? ☐

C ACTING COACH

CONCERNS

- Are the characters different from each other? ☐
- Do the actors show reactions and decisions on their face and through their physical movements? ☐
- Do the actors show a whole range of emotions for their characters? ☐
- Are the performances subtle and underplayed to make the most of the emotional impact on the audience? ☐

D DIRECTOR

CONCERNS

- What sort of emotional impact is your Overall Objective going to need? ☐
- How can you provoke the right reaction at the end of the play? ☐
- How will you stage the scenes to help achieve the Overall Objective? ☐
- How will tension be built up in order to create a climax at the end? ☐
- What sound, lights, set and costume can help achieve the Overall Objective? ☐

Think about the overall purpose of this drama – your Overall Objective. What reactions do you want to provoke from the audience? These will help you create your Overall Objective.

What ideas have you had that might help you achieve this Overall Objective?

Good luck, as you now start to devise your own drama with these things in mind!

The Choice

Characters: Kevin, Mara, Anna, Kate, Mark, Paul

Scene One

We are in a darkened room. There are five friends waiting in the room who can be seen in the dim light. Most of the following dialogue is whispered and urgent, as they all stare at the door, waiting.

Kevin: Where's Mark? The idiot! He's missing his own bleedin' party!

Anna: Remember those headaches of his? He's at the doctors.

Kevin: Yeah, great way to celebrate your birthday.

Kate: *And* he doesn't know we're here. Hence the 'surprise' part of 'surprise birthday party'...

Kevin: Ok, ok. But the footy's on in a minute and I don't wanna miss it!

KATE looks at him angrily and he holds up his hands and stops talking.

Paul: *[trying to break the atmosphere]* What've you all got him?

Mara: That DVD he was after. 'The return of the killer'... something or other. You know, his usual hack and slash stuff.

Paul: That's the third one, right?

Mara: Is it? Oh, I thought I'd bought the second. How many are there? Oh, damn, you've got me all worried now.

Kate: Nah, he won't mind. He'll watch anything twice. We got him a t-shirt.

Kevin: Did we? *[sarcastic]* Wow, he'll be 'so' pleased.

Kate: With 'Good Luck for the Marathon' on it.

Mara: Wonderful idea! He'll love that.

Anna: *[quietly]* You always think of such great presents.

Kevin: *[reluctantly]* It's ok, I suppose. For a girl-thing.

KATE hits him without looking at him. PAUL suddenly 'shh's' everyone as the door begins to open.

MARK enters looking haggard and down.

ALL: Surprise!

PAUL switches on the lights and the five are stood there staring at him. MARK stares back, blinking in the light and smiling only slightly.

Mark: Hey, guys, you remembered. This is so... kind. Thank you.

Kevin: *[stepping forward and slapping him on the shoulder]* **Anything for you mate. And you'll love the present I got you.** *[he looks to KATE, who is scowling]* **We got you, I mean.**

Mark: Will I? Great. That's really great of you. All of you.

 Everyone knows what a surprise birthday party is like. This opening scene helps the audience connect, resonate, with the characters from the start. (Session 1)

D The hook here is the way Mark doesn't react as the audience expects to 'surprise'. Make this a real contrast and the audience will be intrigued! (Session 1)

Anna: [stepping forward] **What's wrong?**

Everyone falls silent and there's a real awkward tension in the air as suddenly no one is quite sure where to look.

MARK moves to the sofa and sits down slowly. ANNA sits next to him and takes his hand. ANNA looks to her friends, scared, and then back to MARK. He meets her gaze and then sees she is scared and straightens up.

Mark: **Good and bad news, I guess…** [no one dares to breathe and MARK looks away, unable to sound at all funny]. **Bad news is that there won't be another one of these surprise parties. Good news is that it'll save you money on birthday presents for me. You won't need to anymore.**

With this he rubs his face with his hands, trying to hold it together. ANNA just stares at him, in deep shock. She tries to take his hand but MARK won't let her. She shakes her head, stands and grabs her coat, tears in her eyes. ANNA is about to say something to MARK as she's at the door, but shakes her head and leaves.

C Even in this short scene the audience should get a sense of the range of characters involved in the story from their reactions. (Session 1)

Scene Two

We are in the common room of a sixth form. KATE and KEVIN have their books out but aren't really working.

Kate: **Yes, but why do you have to keep making jokes about it? Anna's upset enough as it is!**

Kevin: **Everyone's being so bloody depressed about it. Mark's ill. Big deal. He can use the NHS Card he got yesterday for his birthday. Treatment! End of story.**

Kate: [sighing] **Yeah, you're right, I know. It's just…**

Kevin: **You think there's something else wrong between Anna and Mark? Isn't it just Anna's mum? That's enough to get anyone down.**

MARA enters and runs up to them.

Mara: **Heard anything from Anna? Is she in today? How's Mark?**

Kate: **Slow down, Mara. In order – no, nothing from Anna, don't know how she is and Mark's not saying much. He was just with me in Maths and didn't even look at me.**

Mara: **So, has he been to the doctor's again? When's the treatment scheduled?**

Kate: [grabbing her friend's frantic hands] **Hey, Mara, I don't know. Calm down, you're only going to make it worse. Just… relax, will you?**

MARK enters the common room and spots them, pauses as though he's going to go back out and then heads over.

Mark: **Hiya guys. Look, I'm sorry about yesterday. I shouldn't have…**

Kevin: **Alright, mate, don't make me cry now. Sorry is fine. Let's move on. When the hell is your treatment?**

S This scene sets up that not everyone feels the same way about how Mark should deal with things… This leads to conflict, which leads to tension. (Session 2)

D 'Relax, will you?' is a part of the rhythm of this scene. It starts to build in tension and this line puts the audience on pause until the next build–up. (Session 2)

S storyteller **C** acting coach **D** director

Mark:	Have you seen Anna? Any of you?
Mara:	I was just asking that. Is something wrong? She was really upset. Is it her mum again as well as you?
Kate:	*[cutting in to stop MARA]* When did you last see her, Mark?
Mark:	Yesterday. When she left.
Mara:	And you know why she left, don't you, you just don't want to tell us.
Mark:	Mara, please. That's not it. It's just a promise I made to Anna. I can't tell you unless she let's me.
	KEVIN leans forward and takes his NHS Card out of his wallet.
Kevin:	*[a little angry]* **Listen again to my question, Mark. When are you going to use this?** *[he waves the NHS Card in MARK's face]* **You didn't answer me.**
Mark:	I'm going to be fine, Kev. Stop hassling me.
Kevin:	Hassling? You're so ill you may not be here next year, so you claim…
Mark:	*[standing and getting angry himself]* **'Claim!' What's that supposed to mean?**
Mara:	No, don't do this, you two. Please, just listen to each other.
Kate:	Mara, shut your whinging for once. Kevin, sit down and grow up.
	KEVIN doesn't look at KATE but is about to do as she asks when MARK speaks again.
Mark:	Yeah, be the obedient dog like you always are. *[MARK regrets his words straightaway but it's too late judging by KEVIN and KATE's reactions]*
Kevin:	*[really beginning to lose it]* **The only reason I'm not smacking your teeth down your throat is because I love Kate too much for her to see it. Mark, 'mate', I'm going to put that one down to stress. But not a second time. Now get your damn Card out and bloody well go back to that quack and get some treatment.**
Mark:	I can't.
Mara:	Mark, of course you can. They'll see you straightaway – you know how good the system is these days.
Mark:	I can't.
Kate:	*[still angry but restrained]* **Is this something else you won't tell us? Or perhaps you'd like to insult Kevin again to make you feel better? What is going…?**
Mark:	I've given it away! Alright? I've given it away already. I haven't got a Card anymore so I can't go and get any of your wonderful bloody treatment. Are you happy now?
	He stares at them for a beat. Then his face crumples and KATE moves to him and hugs him tightly as he cries in fear.

C Kevin's question about the Card will be on the audience's mind here, as well. This will make them look at the other characters' reactions, so make them count! (Session 2)

Scene Three

We are in ANNA's bedroom. She is sat by her mirror, brushing her hair absently. Her music is playing in the background on her CD player. She stares in the mirror. As she does so MARK appears behind her on the other side of the stage.

Mark: Well, it's good news and bad news, I guess you could say...

MARK laughs.

ANNA shakes her head and turns to face MARK but he's gone. PAUL is standing there instead. ANNA starts to walk towards him.

Paul: Hey, sis. You're not still expecting him to open up, are you? How many times have I told you? He doesn't care about you. He's only after one thing. I won't let him treat my only sister that way. Stuff him. He's better off dead.

PAUL laughs as well. His light goes down.

Anna: No, he's better than that. I remember when we first...

MARK steps into the light, crouching down as though about to run on a track.

Mark: Out of the way, please, genius at work.

ANNA jumps at his appearance and steps to the side.

Anna: Sorry, I was just looking at the track. I've just arrived at the college and wanted to take up some sport.

Mark: *[straightening up]* Really? I'm training for the marathon, would you believe? I can always use a running partner.

Anna: Running... Hmm... Sounds good. *[she smiles]*

Mark: Keep smiling at me like that and I'll run the marathon for you now, let alone next year. *[his light goes down and ANNA is on her own]*

Paul: *[appearing briefly for one word]* Corny.

Anna: Sincere. He'd always say things like that. But he'd really mean them.

PAUL shakes his head and waves ANNA away before disappearing.

Mara: *[appearing and continuing to do ANNA's hair]* So, what's he like, this new bloke of yours?

Anna: Amazing. *[MARA smiles]* No, I mean it, really amazing. So funny, warm and caring.

Mara: But?

Anna: He keeps everyone away. You know, just at a distance.

MARK appears and hands over a bunch of flowers with a quick kiss on the cheek for ANNA before grinning and heading off-stage.

Mara: *[stepping into a light]* He's lovely, Anna. Go on, if you don't want him, I'll take him off your hands. I'm not so proud I won't take second-hand goods.

MARA smiles a sad, lonely smile before she steps back into the darkness.

D This scene is non-naturalistic. How unusual can you make the staging so that it still remains clear to the audience what is going on in Anna's mind? (Session 3)

C The way Anna reacts in the stage directions helps us to realise we are seeing her thoughts. (Session 3)

 storyteller   acting coach   director

Anna: Thanks, but I want to keep this one. You should have seen what he did when…

Paul: *[looking nervous and sad]* **Oh, God, Anna, I've got to talk to you. Mum told me I couldn't tell you. Said you were too young. But it's only a couple of years, right? And… forgive me, Annie, but I just can't keep this to myself. I wish dad were still with us. I miss him, don't you? He'd know what to do.** *[taking a deep breath and then looking at ANNA straight in the eyes]* **Mum's had some tests done. You know how her breathing's got worse?** *[he tries to make a joke of it]* **All that smoking, as she says. Well, the tests are back and…** *[he can't finish, just shakes his head]*. **I'm sorry, sis, but she needs proper treatment and we haven't got a single Card in the family.**

The lights go immediately down on PAUL and straight up on MARK.

Mark: **Hah! Is that all?**

MARK smiles easily and reaches into his wallet. With an elaborate bow he flourishes his NHS Card and hands it to ANNA.

Mark: **It arrived this morning with the birthday cards. Your mum needs it more than I do. They're only headaches I've got. It's nothing. Here.**

Anna: *[deeply moved]* **I love you, Mark.**

MARK just smiles and looks awkward.

Suddenly ANNA is woken by her brother, PAUL, calling her name. MARK's light goes out.

Paul: **Hey, sis, you're meant to get into bed before you sleep, you know.** *[his smile isn't very convincing]*

Anna: **What do you want, Paul? Why're you in my room?** *[he doesn't answer and she sits up, alarmed]* **What's wrong?**

Paul: *[finding this difficult]* **Mara's just phoned. Mark said at college today that he's already given his NHS Card away. He can't get treatment.**

Anna: *[closing her eyes as an image of MARK appears behind her, bowing as he gives her his NHS Card]* **I know, Paul. I know who he gave it to.** *[she sighs]* **Come here, I've got something to tell you.**

PAUL sits down next to her and the music covers the rest of the dialogue as PAUL hears the story she tells.

S This speech by Paul shows a lot of his and Anna's characters' background. This must have been a horrible moment for Anna's character, so it needs to have *resonance* for the audience to feel the same way. (Session 3)

D This change here is back into naturalistic staging. Make sure the audience realise they are watching 'normal' time again, not in Anna's mind. (Session 3)

Scene Four

The following is a montage scene showing different elements of the characters' lives over a number of months. Fast-paced music plays over this scene until indicated.

PAUL stands sharply from ANNA and is clearly angry at her news. He shakes his head and points at the far side of the stage where MARK is standing. PAUL leaves angrily.

ANNA turns to MARK with a smile and he smiles tentatively at her and then winces. ANNA runs to him and he pushes her away. We see KEVIN in the background watching as ANNA backs off confused.

When ANNA moves to the side of the stage, looking upset but angry, KEVIN moves next to MARK and pats him on the shoulder. With his other hand KEVIN produces his wallet and flips out his NHS Card, offering it to MARK. MARK pretends his pain isn't as bad and shakes his head, walking away.

KEVIN is left there, with Card in hand. KATE enters with KEVIN's coat and scarf. It's now clearly cold weather and KEVIN accepts the coat, shaking his head when KATE asks with her face 'how that went?' KATE offers him a cup of coffee and they move off stage as MARA watches forlornly from the side.

MARA is wrapped in winter clothes with study books in her hands. She sits down at a desk, blowing heat into her hands. PAUL turns up late and drops his own books next to her. MARA is delighted to see him and they both chat about the work as ANNA watches from another side of the stage, urging her friend to ask her brother out.

MARA sees ANNA urging her on and turns shyly to PAUL but doesn't manage to ask the question. MARA stands, upset, and walks off quickly, shaking her head at ANNA as she passes her.

This sequence is repeated as though in springtime. Different clothes are worn by the characters to emphasise the passage of time.

The links are the same pairings – ANNA tries to explain to PAUL, who doesn't want to listen; MARK goes to offer ANNA a bunch of spring flowers but drops them when his headache kicks in, this time it doesn't pass as quickly and he dabs at his nose as though it is running with blood; ANNA is upset at this and won't take the flowers from him, exiting in anger; KATE enters as MARK is left on stage with the flowers and takes them from him – KATE rolls her eyes at MARK and pushes past him, taking the flowers with her to catch up with ANNA; KEVIN comes on stage to join MARK. They both sit down on the sofa with their feet up. MARK suddenly sits up, spilling the popcorn he was holding. KEVIN hands him a tissue as though it's normal behaviour now. KEVIN wearily offers his NHS Card and MARK angrily pushes it away. MARK exits and KATE collects an ever-increasingly upset KEVIN.

ANNA enters and sees them move to the side of the stage.

PAUL enters the stage and sees his sister watching KEVIN and KATE.

MARA enters the stage some distance behind PAUL and watches both him and her friend, ANNA.

S Mark is the centre of all these moments. That's why they were chosen. Either he is there, or characters are reacting to his condition. (Session 4)

D See how the suggestion for clothes may help the audience see that time has passed? What other ways can you show the audience they are seeing months go by? (Session 4)

C Kevin is shown becoming more and more frustrated at Mark. This shows a growth and development in his character. This is his arc in this montage. (Session 4)

 storyteller   **acting coach**   **director**

MARK enters in running gear, whilst everyone else freezes in the tableaux as described.

MARK runs to the front and centre of the stage and then has a stabbing pain in his head, ending in him kneeling down, holding his temple. He freezes.

MARA stays watching PAUL. KATE turns to watch KEVIN as he walks to meet ANNA in the middle of the stage, up stage of where MARK is kneeling, frozen.

Kevin: *[gesturing to the frozen MARK]* **What the hell kind of friend do you think I am? I've been trying for months. I've found him a Card, Anna. Mine. He can have it. That's what friends are for, right? But it's him. He's just too proud to take the damn thing.**

ANNA looks at him and touches his arm in apology.

Anna: **Come to my house in half an hour. This has gone on too long.**

ANNA doesn't look at anyone before she exits.

Kate: **Well, if Mark isn't ill now, he sure will be when she gets hold of him.**

Kevin: *[quietly]* **Good luck, Anna.**

Everyone freezes as the lights drop to blackout.

Scene Five

MARA and ANNA in ANNA's living room.

Mara: **But why? It makes no sense. Why wouldn't he take it? Kev's happy to give his up and none of us have a Card left.**

ANNA shrugs her shoulders.

Anna: **I don't know. He's shut down again. Just like he always does.**

Mara: *[quietly and with feeling]* **It must be frustrating feeling like you do and not knowing what's on his mind.**

Anna: *[moving to her friend]* **Oh, Mara, this can't be easy for you. You'll find someone, I know you will.**

Mara: *[smiling]* **I've just got to ask them first?**

Anna: **Well, yeah, that would help.**

They smile at each other.

There's an alerting knock at the front door and then MARK enters the room, putting his front door keys away. There is a moment's awkward silence.

Mark: **You texted me. Here I am.**

Mara: **I think there's some tea burning somewhere.**

Anna: *[looking at her]* **Thanks, Mara, but stay here, will you, please? I could do with the help.**

D The scene begins part-way through already. Can you split it up in another order to increase the tension for the audience? You could start at the final moments and then replay this section so that audience see how it began. This is cross-cutting… (Session 5)

Mark: What's this about?

Anna: *[going over to him and taking his hand]* We've spent nearly six months dancing around this. And I think you and I are going to finish if you don't tell me what's going on.

Mark: *[realising]* Kevin's Card.

Anna: *Anyone's* Card. I don't care whose Card you take. Just get treatment.

Mark: How's your mum?

Anna: *[breaking contact with him]* Oh, that's low. That's a really cheap shot.

Mark: I just meant… I just wanted to know…wanted to know that she was alright.

Anna: *[shouting]* Thank you! Is that what you want to hear? Thank you!

Mark: Stop it. Stop it!

PAUL enters the room.

Paul: I heard shouting – oh, it's you. Haven't you done enough?

Mark: *[turning away]* Don't you start.

Paul: As far as Anna's concerned, Mark, I'll do whatever it takes to protect her. I know what you did for mum, but Anna's my family as well. Might be worth remembering that.

There is a look between MARK and PAUL. MARK looks away first.

KATE and KEVIN enter the room suddenly and cheerfully.

Kate: Hi. No one answered.

Kevin: Can we come in? Don't want to miss Mark's excuses this time. *[there's no humour just bitterness in this comment]*

Mark: We've been through this, Kev. It's your Card and you might need it. I'll get a new one soon.

Kevin: That's right, mate, with at least four months before your next birthday.

Kate: All this for one treatment, Mark.

Mark: But it's Kev's Card!

Kevin: *[frustrated]* Which means I've got the right to give it away!

Mara: *[suddenly realising and speaking up for the first time]* You're scared, aren't you? Scared it won't work. It's better to run away and know for sure it won't work than to try it out and have it fail.

ANNA touches MARA's shoulder in sympathetic understanding.

Mark: Why are you all doing this?

Kevin: Scared? That's what this is all about? You, the great Marathon runner, scared of getting some treatment that will probably save your bloody life!

(S) Mark's line is not nice but the audience need to understand how defensive and upset he is when he makes it. That way they will *still* feel sorry for him. (Session 5)

 storyteller   acting coach **D** director

Mark: Don't you dare judge me! You can't know what it's like. I wake up every day wondering how bad the headache's going to be today. How blurred my vision is or how many times I'll be sick. Every single day! You want me to try some treatment that makes me worse? That 'might' work! It's bad enough now and you want me to just dig in and put up with it? No way.

Anna: Here's a newsflash for you, Mark... You **are** going to die. Behaving like this, some people will think you're probably **better off dead** [*she glares at PAUL, who looks away guiltily*]. **Your mum and dad are going to die someday. All of us are. Even my mum, our mum, is going to die. And we've already lost dad. But you know what? It happens. I can't stand to watch it, but it doesn't change the facts. You've given mum an extra year, I reckon, but she's still going to die. You are going to die sooner or later. You're not unique. You're not that special. Your heart will stop one day and we'll be sticking you in the ground and crying all over you. I'd like that time to be many, many years after my mum's gone, but, hey, why should she crowd out your moment of glory, right? Don't you get it Mark? We love you. I love you!**

There is a silence so still that you couldn't push it aside.

Kevin: So, what're you going to do, Mark? Sit there in your pool of self-pity or get off your marathon-trained backside and swallow your damn pride?

Anna: It's your choice.

KEVIN is standing to one side, hand reaching out with the NHS Card in it. ANNA is staring fiercely at MARK. MARK looks from ANNA to KEVIN and then the Card.

The lights fade before MARK moves.

C These two speeches are very emotional. The audience will be looking carefully to see how every other character reacts during different parts of these speeches. Make sure we can see what they all think at every line. (Session 5)

D This ending could be the *start* of the scene. We might see this first as a freeze-frame and then the beginning of the scene takes place leading to this moment. That way the audience feels a sense of tension by cross-cutting the scene. (Session 5)

Scene Six

We are at a party again. From the signs and cards everywhere it is a birthday party for MARK. However, MARK is missing. The other five characters are sat around in a living room. This is much like the very first scene, but with a much tenser atmosphere. No one is speaking and no one is looking at each other.

KEVIN looks round at everyone else. He picks up a drink and sadly raises it in the air.

Kevin: To Mark.

KATE looks at him in disgust for a moment and then sees that he's not joking. She smiles and nods, raising her own drink.

Kate: OK. To Mark.

Everyone else joins in quietly.

Mara: [*quietly*] Wherever he is now.

Anna: He's…

ANNA can't talk anymore. She covers her face with her hands and starts to cry. MARA leans over and puts her arm around her.

Mara: It's alright, Anna. It's going to be okay.

Anna: No, it's not! Don't say that! We all know it's not. Why him? Why? Can any of you tell me that? Look at us. We're sat here 'celebrating' his birthday and where is he? Why can't it have been me? Or Kevin? Or any of us? What did he ever do wrong that he needed punishing for? This just isn't…

The door opens and MARK walks in.

Mark: Fair?

There is a moment's awkwardness from everyone.

Anna: Yeah. It's not fair. I know that sounds stupid, but it's not.

There is a long pause and then MARK looks to ANNA.

Mark: Some things have a way of working out, though, don't you think?

Everyone's head turns to him at this remark. MARK's eyes are glittering, with a hidden smile creeping from the corner of his mouth.

Kate: You got the results?

MARK nods, his smile tumbling out now.

Mark: They're clear. I'm clear. It's over.

There is a moment's stunned silence. Suddenly the room erupts into noise and movement. MARK is mobbed by everyone, hugging him, cheering and slapping him on the back. There are not many dry eyes.

KEVIN grins broadly, grabbing MARK's hand and shaking it furiously. MARK thanks him gently and then looks over to the other side of the room.

We see MARA grab PAUL's hand and squeeze it. PAUL reacts surprised and then smiles and squeezes her hand back.

ANNA is the only one who hasn't moved. She stands on the opposite side of the group and looks at MARK with tears running down her face. The room falls silent and MARK moves over to her. He faces her and wipes away a few of her tears.

Anna: I thought… *[she shakes her head, unable to say it out loud].* I thought you weren't coming back to us. To me. *[she smiles at herself]*

Mark: And miss that smile?

They kiss and then hug. He breaks the hug as everyone else tries not to watch. MARK turns to his friends.

Mark: *[really moved]* Hey, guys… *[he shrugs]* I don't know what to say. Thanks doesn't seem enough. But that's all I've got.

Ⓢ It should be clear from the script that this play is about friendship and what we are prepared to do for love. That is its Overall Objective and this scene, particularly when Mark enters when the audience least expect it, is the emotional high-point of that message.
(Session 6)

Ⓒ This is a really emotional scene, and these lines here particularly. They are written with a lot of emotion so they can be played with a lot of subtlety. This **under-playing** will mean the audience feels even more emotion.
(Session 6)

 storyteller   **acting coach**   Ⓓ **director**

Kevin: Fine. That'll do. Now stop this emotional crap and open the damn presents, will you?

Mark: *[laughing but grateful]* Yeah, you're right. I want to see what rubbish film Mara's got me.

Mara: Oh, shut up, else you won't get anything.

Mark: OK, come on. Load me up. Give me prezzies! Lots of them. For a long time yet!

His friends come to him, producing their presents. KATE produces another T-shirt for him, with the words 'Marathon Runners Go The Distance.' MARK laughs and carries on opening the other presents with enthusiasm.

Slowly the lights fade as the friends gather and MARK continues to open his presents.

The End

D Notice how the t-shirt prop is used as a symbol to show the audience Mark's success. It is also a prop that the audience can connect with and produces emotional resonance as a result.
(Session 6)

Unit 4 The Choice

Glossary

The following are brief definitions of some of the words and phrases used in this book. Some words have common-use definitions but the ones that follow are given the meanings found in drama.

Acting Coach – the person responsible for making sure every actor is performing to the best of their ability and communicating their character to the audience effectively and emotionally.

Ad-libbing – when actors make up lines. This can be used in a script when characters are saying 'hello' or 'goodbye' – it's no use scripting every single one of these, so a writer will allow an actor to think what would work best for their character.

Arc – the way a complete character is shown to an audience throughout a play or performance. A good arc is when a character starts off a play with one set of beliefs or feelings and finishes the play with another set. This way you are showing the audience a range.

Atmosphere – creating an emotional feeling in the audience so that they are ready to take on the message and overall objective. A spooky atmosphere can be set by the director using music and sound effects, for example.

Audience – the most important people in drama! Well, apart from the actors, perhaps! The audience are who you perform for, they are the ones you create the drama for and the people you want to affect. So, fairly important people, really!

Background – when your character has a history which affects what they do. There's no point in mentioning to an audience that your character didn't like having his hair cut when he was six if it has no effect on the story you are telling when the character is twenty! *Relevant* background helps an audience understand a character.

Blocking (three separate meanings!)

1. When an actor stands in front of another actor, masking them from the audience (not a good thing!).

2. When a director moves actors around the stage so they know where to move and why to move there (this is a good thing!).

3. When you stop an improvisation from continuing by not allowing the ideas to flow (not a good thing, either!). So, only number 2 is something you should aim for!

Body language – the way we stand as characters can tell the audience who we are and what we are thinking. Arms folded is usually defensive, head raised can mean defiance, etc.

Character – the person you are creating when you, the actor, step on stage to impress, impact and affect the audience.

Comedy – a play which makes the audience laugh (hopefully).

Commitment – a skill you need as Storyteller, Acting Coach, Director or student, to see you through the tough times when not everything goes right.

Communication – the ability to explain ideas, thoughts and feelings to your group and then to the audience.

Conflict – the source of all good drama! If all the characters on stage get on, then the audience isn't going to want to watch.

Context – the setting or background of an idea. If two characters disagree about keeping a dog, the context is 'because they live in a flat 20 floors above ground level!'

Glossary

Contrast – changing from one extreme to another. Good contrast is essential to all drama. Shakespeare was a master of it – changing a serious moment in a play to comedy. Contrast can mean fast to slow, slow to fast, scary to funny or any one thing to its opposite.

Counterpoint – when one idea is presented with its exact opposite at the same time.

Creativity – the ability to think original thoughts.

Dialogue – the spoken part of a script. Dialogue – the lines that characters say to one another in a script.

Director – the person responsible for staging a play, for moving the actors in a particular way, for creating the set, the mood, the pace and the effect! No small job, this...

Drama – good drama comes from conflict. Drama is when two characters don't agree. Drama is what makes us watch the stage, television and film.

Dress rehearsal – the final rehearsal before the play is on. A dress rehearsal is always done with full costume, lights and sound and NO stops! In other words, as per a performance.

Duologue – when two characters have a chat together.

Effect – the change in an audience's emotions because of the play they have seen. This is the effect you are having on them.

Evaluation – the ability to tell what is working about a play (and why) and what needs changing to make it work even better (and why!).

Evoke – forcing an effect on a person, or an audience. Making them react in the way that you want.

Factors – elements that help you make a choice.

Focus – where the audience should be looking at any one time on stage. A good director knows exactly where an audience should be looking when every scene of a play is taking place.

Foreshadowing – dropping hints to an audience about what might happen later in a play. Having a gun in the first scene, for example, might make them think it will be used later in the play.

Freeze-frames – when actors stop moving and hold a 'pose' like a photograph.

Hook – what grabs the audience and keeps them watching after the opening scene.

Hot-seating – a rehearsal technique which allows actors to question each other in role. They perform as their character and the other actors ask them questions.

Impact – the memorable events which take place in a play that leave a mental or emotional dent in the audience's mind or heart.

Intention – what you, as a group, set out to do. How you want to affect an audience's heart and mind.

Levels – a director's term which means making sure that actors aren't all sat down, or all stood up. The more varied a group of characters are on stage (some sat, some leaning, some moving, some standing still) gives the stage levels and makes it look more interesting for the audience.

Glossary

Mark the moment – using a range of techniques so that the audience is forced to see something significant and realise that it is significant.

Monologue – when one actor is on stage and speaking. Usually, but not always, to the audience.

Monotone – speaking in a flat, lifeless voice with no inflection. This is only recommended when you are trying to go for a particular effect on the audience (sending them to sleep, presumably!)… otherwise put as much life and range in your voice as possible!

Mood – what feelings you evoke in the audience with a certain scene or a whole play.

Motive – the reason a character has for doing something. You always try and show (or explain) to an audience why a character is doing something. If a woman walks into a chemist and hands them a drum, you have to explain to the audience that she has hiccups and wants the chemist to bang the drum to shock her out of the hiccups! Motive (and motivation) is connected to the background of a character.

Narrative – the story which goes through a play. The sequence of events which make up the story.

Narrative drive – what forces the story events to take place. For example, if your character has an illness which needs a cure, then the narrative drive is their search for that cure. It's what drives the story along.

Naturalistic – performing a play in as 'real' a way as you can.

Non-naturalistic – performing a play in a way that an audience would not normally be used to, or which allows them to see things they wouldn't normally be able to (for example, inside a character's mind).

Originality – not copying off the television, a book or films. Originality keeps an audience guessing, wondering what is going on and what will happen next. This keeps your play fresh and new.

Overall Objective – the intention you have towards the audience. What do you want them to think about and how do you want them to feel during and at the end of your play? This is the Overall Objective. Every scene you ever create should feed into the agreed Overall Objective.

Pace – this is the change of speed of the action on stage. Do not confuse this with going fast! Pace is when things change from slow to fast or fast to slow. The more pace – the more change – the more involved the audience will become.

Pause – when the action halts for a moment or the actors take a breath in the dialogue to react and let the audience see them react to one another. Too many pauses can be boring, but too few and the audience is lost. You have to balance this, directors!

Pitch – the tone of your voice, whether it is high, low or middling. The more range you use in your voice, the more interesting your character is to the audience.

Plot – the events which happen in a set order for your play.

Projection – pushing your voice so that all of the audience can hear you clearly even when you might whisper.

Prop (short for properties) – the hand-held objects that help create a character (jewellery, glasses, sweets, etc.).

Glossary

Reactions – the ability of an actor to use their face and body to show an audience what their character is thinking even when they're not speaking at that moment. The best actors are the best reactors.

Relationships – how one character gets on with another character. Just as in real life, all relationships change with age and time. So should yours in any of your plays, so long as there is a reason for the change.

Rhythm – the ebb and flow of the action, pace or tension in a scene or a play. Good rhythm means good change.

Scene – a series of dramatic moments that usually (but not always) take place in a single location. A scene is a short sequence of drama, forming part of a whole (a play).

Scene change – when props and furniture are changed in front of the audience.

Stage Directions – upstage is furthest from the audience, downstage is nearest, stage left is to the audience's right (!) and stage right is to the audience's left.

Staging – how you place the actors, the set and the furniture on stage.

Status – how one character's power is shown to the audience. Status is when one person feels they are more, or less, important than another. A good example of this is a boss and an employee. Usually, a boss has more status and an employee has less.

Stimulus – what starts an idea, or the beginnings of a play.

Story – the sequence of events that form a narrative with a purpose to entertain and affect an audience.

Storyteller – the person who thinks up the sequence of events that make up a play.

Structure – in what order a sequence of events takes place to give the most dramatic impact on the audience (and so meet the needs of the Overall Objective).

Style – is the play naturalistic, non-naturalistic, comedy, drama, etc.? In what way is the play performed?

Subtle – small events, reactions or situations. Not going over the top!

Teamwork – working together with a group of people, even when you don't get on with them all (and this happens a lot in drama with different ideas flying around!).

Tech (technical) – the lights, sound and stage-management of a show.

Telegraphing – hinting to the audience about a character's thoughts or feelings through subtle means.

Tension – making an audience want to see what happens next. Suspense!

Thriller – a style of play that, through action, grips the audience from start to finish.

Volume – the loudness of your voice when you perform. This does not always have to be very loud, but it does have to be loud enough to be heard by everyone in the audience!

CERTIFICATE
OF
ACHIEVEMENT

Name --

Class ---------------------------- Date --------------

This certificate recognises the considerable
achievements of a hard-working and committed
student in Drama in their role as

STORYTELLER

Your work in organising your group's ideas
to make clear their Intention, identify the Conflict
and Plot the structure of the piece
has been brilliant!

Congratulations!

Signed for the Drama Dept.

CERTIFICATE
OF
ACHIEVEMENT

Name --

Class -------------------------- Date --------------

This certificate recognises the considerable
achievements of a hard-working and committed
student in Drama in their role as

ACTING COACH

Your work in developing the characterisations
of your group, helping to create the right Effect,
Character Arc and Physical Skills
has been brilliant!

Congratulations!

Signed for the Drama Dept.

CERTIFICATE
OF
ACHIEVEMENT

Name _____

Class _____ Date _____

This certificate recognises the considerable achievements of a hard-working and committed student in Drama in their role as

DIRECTOR

Your work in directing your group's work, helping create Impact, show Tension and consider Staging has been brilliant!

Congratulations!

Signed for the Drama Dept.

Index

Index

Index

Index